PRAISE FOR *KEEP THE FAITH*

"In a day of trendy trails and nondescript names, Dr. Chappell encourages us to ponder the path of our feet and to embrace our biblical heritage as Baptists. *Keep the Faith* is a clarion call to faithfulness, and all of us would do well to read and heed. I love the author, I love the book, and I love the spirit in which it was written."
Dean Herring, Pastor, South Valley Baptist Church,
Kuna, Idaho

"This book is not the result of a few hours or days; it has been lived over a lifetime. I'm thankful Dr. Chappell wrote it. I'm thankful for the thought and prayer he has put into it. And I believe it will have a great influence for the good of the gospel."
Don Sisk, Director Emeritus, Baptist International Missions, Inc.
Chairman of Missions Department, West Coast Baptist College,
Lancaster, California

"*Keep the Faith* is a must read for every believer and every spiritual leader. In these pages, Dr. Chappell gives a clear call for biblical ministry. This is sound direction from someone who has walked this road for decades."
Dean Miller, Pastor, Front Range Baptist Church,
Fort Collins, Colorado

"Throughout *Keep the Faith*, Dr. Chappell maintains an emphasis on the truth of God's Word and encourages each reader to stand true to the fundamental doctrines of the Bible. This book is both informational and instructional as he reminds us of our heritage and calls us back to the God of our fathers."
Tim Rabon, Pastor, Beacon Baptist Church,
Raleigh, North Carolina

"*Keep the Faith* is a window into the heart for pastors and Christian ministry workers that Pastor Chappell has modeled for decades. I am convinced that this book will transform the way you lead in ministry."
Dave Delaney, Pastor, First Baptist Church,
Long Beach, California

"*Keep the Faith* challenges a new generation of Bible-believers to take a strong and gracious stand for the truth. Dr. Chappell makes a compelling case for biblical separation while navigating the complexities of contemporary trends. *Keep the Faith* will prompt needed changes within our movement."
Tyler Gillit, Pastor, Worth Baptist Church,
Fort Worth, Texas

"I appreciate and admire Pastor Chappell's continual investments to influence the next generation of Christian servants. In these pages, you will find reasoned, biblical, and needed instruction for pastors and Christian servants in this generation and the generations to follow. May God use this book to help a multitude of men and women who desire to keep the faith for a lifetime!"
Ryan Thompson, Pastor, Liberty Baptist Church,
Newport Beach, California

"Some books are helpful. Some are challenging. Some are timely. A few are timeless. Dr. Paul Chappell's new book *Keep the Faith* is all of these. It may be the most important book written in a generation. It is certainty vital for our generation and those to come. Every pastor who loves the truth should read this invaluable book."
R. B. Ouellette, Pastor Emeritus, First Baptist Church,
Bridgeport, Michigan

"Remember the advertisement, 'When E. F. Hutton talks, people listen'? Well, when Dr. Paul Chappell writes, I read! This excellent book gives a helpful, historical summary of vital Baptist history, current issues trending in Baptist circles, and a way forward for sincere believers and faithful Baptist churches. I encourage you to read it carefully. It will help you to keep the faith."
Jerry Vines, Previous President of the
Southern Baptist Convention;
Pastor Emeritus, First Baptist Church,
Jacksonville, Florida

PAUL CHAPPELL

KEEP

THE

FAITH

STANDING FOR BIBLICAL TRUTH

DISCERNING MINISTRY TRENDS

REACHING FORWARD WITH THE GOSPEL

First published in 2020 by Striving Together Publications, a ministry of Lancaster Baptist Church, Lancaster, CA 93535. Striving Together Publications is committed to providing tried, trusted, and proven books that will further equip local churches to carry out the Great Commission. Your comments and suggestions are valued.

All Scripture quotations are taken from the King James Version. Special emphasis in verses is added by the author.

The author and publication team have put forth every effort to give proper credit to quotes and thoughts that are not original with the author. It is not our intent to claim originality with any quote or thought that could not readily be tied to an original source.

Striving Together Publications
4020 E. Lancaster Blvd.
Lancaster, CA 93535
800.201.7748

Cover design: Andrew Jones
Writing assistance: Monica Bass

ISBN 978-1-59894-423-5
ISBN 978-1-59894-429-7 (ebook)

Library of Congress Control Number: 2020941221

Printed in the United States of America

DEDICATION

To my students—past and present—of the
Practical Theology class at West Coast Baptist
College. Your questions prompted this book, your
heart to serve the Lord encourages me, and your
desire to change the world with the
gospel thrills me.

ACKNOWLEDGMENTS

THERE ARE MANY WHO HELPED in the compilation of this project, and I am grateful to each.

I would especially like to thank our West Coast Baptist College administrative and Bible faculty for their review and comments throughout early editions of this book.

Special thanks to Monica Bass and my daughter, Danielle Mordh, of Striving Together Publications for their help with writing and editing.

Finally, thanks to the many pastor friends who reviewed and commented on this manuscript. It is a privilege to labor together with you for the faith of the gospel.

TABLE OF CONTENTS

FOREWORD

BY DAVE DELANEY

L ET ME WARN YOU UP FRONT: while there are many books written to convince you of why you should abandon biblical truth for a more trendy approach to ministry, this is not one of them. Dr. Chappell's work, *Keep the Faith,* is unmatched in terms of its doctrinal richness, biblical commitment, pastoral perspective, and cultural insights.

My first interaction with Pastor Chappell was as a staff member. My wife Amanda and I came to work at Lancaster Baptist at the age of twenty-one. What we saw being put into practice at Lancaster Baptist Church was exactly the kind of ministry philosophy that was rooted in biblical exposition, disciple making, generous hospitality, servant leadership, and soulwinning that we wanted to motivate us.

What I was not prepared for though, was how serving with Pastor Chappell would alter the trajectory of my life from that time forward. I am now thirty-eight years old. I have pastored for just over ten years, and not a day goes by that I do not put into practice the ministry models I learned from Pastor Chappell. I thank God for using Pastor Chappell to help me and so many others understand the significance of striving together for the faith of the gospel. The cumulative impact of his life and ministry will only be revealed in eternity and can only be enjoyed as a gift that God alone gives.

Keep the Faith is a window into the heart for pastors and Christian ministry workers that Pastor Chappell has modeled for decades. Spiritual leaders will be fortified as they benefit from this wisdom at a time when many are wrestling with the external influences and internal pressures to compromise many of the church's long standing tenets. I am convinced that this book will transform the way you lead in ministry. Thanks be to God!

PASTOR DAVE DELANEY
First Baptist Church of Long Beach, California

FOREWORD

BY DON SISK

A LITTLE OVER SIXTY-FIVE YEARS AGO, I preached my first sermon. I have been preaching on a regular basis ever since.

I've had the privilege of serving as a pastor of churches in Kentucky, an associate pastor in Illinois, a missionary in Japan, the Far Eastern Director of Baptist International Missions, Inc. (BIMI), and then as the General Director of BIMI. After my wife Virginia and I "retired," we had the privilege of teaching missions at West Coast Baptist College in Lancaster, California, for well over fifteen years. In recent years, I've had the privilege of continuing to preach in churches, Bible colleges, and conferences all over the world. All that to say, the Lord has enabled me to serve Him for a long time in a variety of capacities, which has led to having a wide perspective of the challenges and trends for gospel-preaching labor.

This generation of Bible believing preachers faces great challenges. And that is why I am grateful Dr. Chappell has written *Keep the Faith.*

When I think back to the early years of my ministry, I was greatly helped by godly pastors and friends in formulating convictions and making decisions that helped me set a direction oriented toward Christ and His truth. Perhaps the greatest challenge in my early ministry was knowing how to respond to the growing modernism in the convention of which I was a member. (Dr. Chappell shares a little of my story from that time in this book.) I'm grateful for the mentors who gave me guidance and helped me through those turbulent times. The challenges of today are largely different from those I faced. But they are not less threatening to the future of a leader's ministry. I believe what Dr. Chappell shares in these pages will be helpful not only to young preachers, but also to older preachers. I'm eighty-seven years old, and it was a great help to me.

Many of the decisions we face in ministry are determined by the convictions that we hold. This is one reason I'm grateful that in the early years of my ministry, the Lord helped me understand principles from Scripture regarding biblical separation. Based on those principles, I have been a Bible-believing separatist for many years now. I'm certainly not an isolationist, but I am a separatist in the sense that there are areas of personal and ecclesiastical separation I have held through the years. Even so, I have never been a fighter. It has been my goal to contend for the faith without being contentious.

This spirit of contending without being contentious is something I have appreciated about Dr. Chappell since I first met him nearly thirty years ago. He was a twenty-something-year-old pastor who had a great heart for souls and was beginning to see the Lord greatly bless the church he was pastoring.

Over the years, the Lord has closely knit Dr. Chappell's and my hearts. It has been my privilege to not only serve together with him as a co-laborer, but also to watch him continue with the same heart, the same focus, and the same convictions in the path on which he started. And it has been my great amazement to watch him continue on this path with deepening wisdom and insight into the various challenges and trends of ministry.

Over the past several years, Dr. Chappell has often mentioned to me his burden for the book you are now reading. This book is not the result of a few hours or days. It has been lived over a lifetime and has been in the making now for some time. I'm thankful he wrote it, I'm thankful for the thought and prayer he has put into it, and I believe it will have a great influence for the good of the gospel.

You may or may not agree with everything that is written here. However, I have always felt that if I could gain something from the writings of others that would help and encourage me, it was worth my time and energy. This book, in particular, is worth your time.

I trust and pray that you will receive this work with the same gracious, prayerful attitude in which it was written.

Dr. Don Sisk

Director Emeritus, Baptist International Missions, Inc.

Chairman of Missions Department, West Coast Baptist College

STRIVING TOGETHER

S INCE THE LORD BROUGHT my wife Terrie and me to Lancaster Baptist Church in July of 1986, our church's theme verse has been Philippians 1:27: "Only let your conversation be as it becometh the gospel of Christ: that whether I come and see you, or else be absent, I may hear of your affairs, that ye stand fast in one spirit, with one mind striving together for the faith of the gospel."

Some years later, when I began hosting preaching and training conferences across the country, I called them "Striving Together Conferences." The website our ministry hosts for collaborative encouragement and resources is ministy127.com, based on the Philippians 1:27 reference about striving together for the gospel. And our church's publishing ministry is named—wait for it—Striving Together Publications.

In case you can't tell, it is my desire to partner with others for the spread of the gospel. I love the heart of the apostle Paul expressed in

Philippians 1 as he implores this church to stand fast in one spirit, with one mind, striving together for the faith of the gospel.

- **One spirit** can only come through the filling of the Holy Spirit within individual Christians. This is true of the spirit within a local church as well as among Christians from various churches.
- **One mind** can only come as individual minds are aligned to the same center—Christ. It is as our minds are saturated with His Word, focused on Him, and embracing His truth that we have unity.
- **One goal**—the faith of the gospel—can only come as we truly make Christ's last command our first priority. Our "striving together" is not for the sake of nebulous unity or simply enjoying camaraderie. It is because together we can do more for the furtherance of the gospel than any of us can do alone.

In recent years, I've been encouraged by the desire among leaders for greater collaboration and striving together. I love pastors and have willingly poured my time and strength into encouraging and helping them into and in the ministry.

In particular, I thank the Lord for the leaders a generation and more younger than me. I see many incredible strengths in these leaders. Those I talk to deeply desire Christ-centered, authentic ministry. They want substance over show. They value teamwork. And while they appreciate past heritage, they want to see greater things in the future. Specifically, they want to reach their generation with the gospel. These qualities thrill my heart.

But at the same time that I'm encouraged by these strengths, I'm troubled by some of the weaknesses, specifically an unwillingness to separate from those whose doctrine is unbiblical. While I'm deeply thankful for the renewed desire among fellow independent Baptists for greater teamwork and unity, I'm concerned by a seeming lack of understanding of or convictions for biblical separation—a principle I'll define more clearly in the coming pages. It has been this concern that has birthed this book.

I started writing this book ten years ago. First a few memos—notes to myself in the midst of wakeful nights. Then a yellow pad, sketching out what should be included and how it should be arranged. Over the following weeks, I tweaked the outline and scribbled out more memos.

I knew this project was vital. I was watching good men, men whom I love and in whom I had invested, walking dangerous bridges of compromise. Some of the sleepless nights were spent in prayer and concern for them.

At one point, my schedule and these concerns along with trials of health in our family became too much to carry. I stepped back to get rest, and I unplugged. I learned to pray more and worry less. Through this experience, the Lord renewed in me a learning how to leave ministry concerns with Him and how to pace myself in service for Him. (The more tangible results were the books *Stewarding Life* and *The Burden Bearer*.)

As I prayed more, I gained both a renewed trust in God and a renewed burden to write this book. That burden has only grown.

Additionally, over the past several years, I've listened more. Although the core content of this book hasn't changed from what it would have been if I had completed and published it ten years ago, I believe I understand better the questions younger leaders are asking. I've had countless discussions with younger men who desire to know *why* rather than to simply be told *what*. They ask good questions and value substantive answers. I appreciate that. I trust this book reflects my heart to listen and come alongside with answers to the questions that are being asked.

Many of the trends and terms we'll discuss in the coming pages first came to my attention through students at West Coast Baptist College asking for my take on them. In the Practical Theology class I teach, I encourage questions and have enjoyed the resulting conversations with young minds who are still forming their ministry philosophy. They see the trends, hear the buzzwords, and want to be sure they are preparing to build a ministry that honors God, is faithful to His Word, and reaches people with the gospel. In part, it has been their questions that have prompted me several times over the past several years to return to this manuscript and both enlarge and complete it.

I've arranged the book in three sections:

- **Part 1: Standing for Biblical Truth**—In these chapters, we look at the importance of truth, the biblical practice of ecclesiastical separation, and the historic practice of those who have stood through the centuries—including the original fundamentalists and then the beginning of the independent Baptist movement.
- **Part 2: Discerning Ministry Trends**—In these chapters, we examine a few current ministry trends—doctrinal and practical—and their strengths and weaknesses.
- **Part 3: Reaching forward with the Gospel**—In these chapters, we look to the future and our commission to reach the world with the gospel.

Another way to break these sections down is this comparison:

- **Part 1**—Ministry *practice.*
- **Part 2**—Ministry *philosophy.*
- **Part 3**—Ministry *motivation.*

This book deals with questions related to keeping the faith in a day when many depart from it, so naturally, the focus of it will lean toward biblical separation. But my heart is for unity and the furtherance of the gospel. Due to the subject matter, my heart to encourage comes through most clearly in the final chapters. I hope you'll stay with me until then.

In the pages that follow, I hope to convey that unity and separation are not opposite ends of a spectrum in which one must find balance, but they are the opposite sides of the same coin that faithful servants of God have held through the centuries. The fact is, biblical separation is not a negative; it is a positive trait that allows for true unity. Separation is not punishment—withholding fellowship until someone conforms to my way; it is a choice to walk with others who are aligned with God's revealed truth.

I have friends who are not independent Baptists. I've been encouraged by many of their books and ministries and, in some cases, a cup of coffee and prayer together. I rejoice in every soul that is saved through the efforts of ministries not just like mine. But all of us have to determine what our ministry philosophy is, who we will allow to deeply influence us, and with whom we will platform and partner.

This book is not advocating separation over preference or personal standards. In fact, it is not even about ministry style or personal standards. Although we will touch on the biblical basis for holiness in our personal lives, I don't argue in this book for the specifics of how that plays out. These are personal and local church issues.

This book is not about me dictating who is "separated enough" or who should preach for whom (as if my opinion even mattered). I don't intend to tell you what you can read or with whom you should fellowship. I recognize the need for each of us to follow the Holy Spirit's leading in these matters.

In some ways, writing a book like this is a no-win. Some may think I'm not specific enough or including enough material on personal separation. Others may think I'm too conservative and criticize my stand as being judgmental. But I'm not writing this book to win; I'm writing to help.

I write primarily to theologically-conservative Christians who share Baptist doctrine and a concern for contending for the faith once delivered to the saints. Anyone who identifies with that statement will hopefully find helpful material. I suppose, however, that even more specifically, I write to younger men in ministry who have been taught or seen some of the issues related to separation, but have questions about how, when, where, why, and if practicing separation is biblical or an isolation strategy sure to kill the power of the gospel. I trust you'll find many of your questions answered in these pages.

In the bibliography, you'll find books with much greater detail and depth than this one, which is in no way exhaustive. I hope you'll reference and read some of the other books I've studied. I will quote in this book from different sides of an issue, including using support quotes from authors I don't agree with on other issues. Some of the quotes I'll use are from men or movements that once stood with much more clarity.

Also, I hope that you'll read this book in context with my previous books. Two are especially relevant: In *Guided by Grace* (which I wrote while in my thirties), I made an appeal for servant leadership among independent Baptists. I encouraged grace-based, rather than fleshly-driven, leadership in the local church as well as in our interactions with one another. In *The Road Ahead,* I wrote about imbalances in independent Baptist ministry and implored a return to humility and unity where there is no doctrinal compromise. I'm not oblivious to the weaknesses among independent Baptists, nor do I consider myself free of weakness or error. But I am grateful for my heritage, and I hope to pass on our biblical practices.

Ultimately, I long for revival in our midst. I don't write to restore "glory days" to a movement. I write to lift up Christ, to join with those who promote and contend for the faith, and to encourage you in the spread of the gospel. To these ends, I pray this book is useful and successful.

PART ONE

STANDING FOR BIBLICAL TRUTH

CHAPTER 1

THE IMPORTANCE
OF THE TRUTH

W E KNOW THAT EVERY WORD of Scripture "is given by inspiration of God" (2 Timothy 3:16), but I will admit that the pastoral epistles are my favorite. In recent years, I've preached verse-by-verse messages through 1 and 2 Timothy and Titus with our church family. But when I had the recent opportunity to visit the island of Crete where Titus was ministering when Paul sent him the epistle written to him, there was one verse in particular that kept coming to mind: "Holding fast the faithful word as he hath been taught, that he may be able by sound doctrine both to exhort and to convince the gainsayers" (Titus 1:9).

No one knows exactly how the gospel first reached Crete. It may have been through the witness of Cretians saved in Jerusalem on the day of Pentecost. It may have been through one of Paul's missionary journeys. (Acts 27:7–8 tells us he stopped at Crete.) But however the gospel first came, there was a lack of sound teaching and doctrine among the

Christians scattered across the island. So Paul left Titus in Crete to "set in order the things that are wanting" (Titus 1:5). I tried to imagine what it must have been like for Titus as Paul charged him with bringing order and leadership to these congregations. And then what it was like for Titus as Paul sailed away.

While visiting Crete, I hired a van to go to the southern part of the island, just north of Libya and Egypt, where we toured the ancient settlement of Gortyn. There we learned of a history that stretches back to at least 1050 BC and includes advanced Minoan settlements and eventually a flourishing and well-fortified Greek city that was the capital of Crete.

In the ruins of the old city, archaeologists discovered the Gortyn Code (or the Great Code), which is the oldest and most complete known example of a written code of ancient Greek law. Carved into the stone wall, its many columns of text are truly impressive to behold.

To me, however, even more amazing than running my fingers along the inscriptions of the Gortyn Code or seeing the ruins of the Basilica of Gordys (a Byzantine church dedicated to Titus and believed to have been built over the place where Titus was martyred), was the enduring legacy of Titus and the pastors he trained. If Titus was indeed martyred, it would be consistent with the legacy he left for other pastors who were also willing to give their lives for Christ.

Titus ministered in Crete around AD 56, and tradition says he continued there longer than half a century, until AD 107. His mission was to train pastors, and as Paul had instructed him, he challenged them to hold "fast the faithful word" that they would "be able by sound doctrine both to exhort and to convince the gainsayers" (Titus 1:9).

The test of faith for Titus's ministry, however, reached beyond his lifetime. In fact, it was AD 250 when the Roman emperor Decius demanded sacrificial worship under the penalty of death for those who refused. The local governor (who was also named Decius) rounded up ten pastors from throughout the island of Greece who refused to obey the edict and had them tortured for thirty days. Their agony was extreme. They were scourged, racked, dragged upon the ground through dung heaps, stoned, spat upon, and starved. When they remained strong in their refusal to worship the emperor, they were martyred.

As I stood outside the old city of Gortyn in the Roman amphitheater where these ten pastors were beheaded, I wondered, "How many years after my preaching ministry will those whom I've led to Christ and their descendants still be keeping the faith?"

Here in America, we've enjoyed religious freedom. Not only is that changing, but our entire culture is following the path of the Romans. Any hope I have for our country lies in my hope for a spiritual revival. Short of a national revival, I believe our country is headed to complete paganism.

So as I stood there where these ten spiritual descendants of Titus were martyred for their faith, I thought of the direction of compromise and entitlement-oriented ministry in America. And I wondered, "Will the teens in our youth groups stand under the pressure of paganism? If the Lord does not return first, will the churches today that are following culturally-approved paths produce Christians whose allegiance to the Lord will be strong enough for martyrdom? Will this trajectory of ministry hold firm 150 years from now?"

Making disciples and building an authentic New Testament church is not about following popular leaders or "shock jock" preaching trends. I believe Titus would tell us that the direction of ministry that will stand the test of time must be the direction of a Christ-centered commitment to biblical truth.

WHY THE TRUTH MATTERS

We enter ministry with a passionate desire to share the truth. We know that the gospel is "the power of God unto salvation to every one that believeth" (Romans 1:16). We preach it, share it one on one, and labor to disciple young Christians and help them become grounded in their faith. We watch the Holy Spirit transform lives through His truth.

But in a world where any claim of absolute truth is despised and where a growing number even of Christians believe that truth itself is too controversial, there is tremendous pressure to position our ministries relative to culture rather than to truth.

But that's not how New Testament Christianity works. The history of the world is a history of man's position to the truth. From the Garden of Eden until now, Satan attacks the truth and deceives hearts through his lies. We who know Christ and hold the truth *must* be committed to it—personally and ecclesiastically. Any ministry endeavor with long-term significance for Christ and lasting fruit will be centered on truth—Jesus Himself and the written Word of God.

In recent decades, post-modernism has been overtaking America. Today, it flourishes to the point that our society is easily and accurately described as a post-Christian society.

What has contributed to this regression? Is it a corrupt government? Is it because the "moral majority" has sunk to a minority? Is it because many of our government leaders no longer publicly affirm Christianity and often belittle Christian values? No, I believe it is because local churches do not stand for the revealed truth of God and have been unwilling to contend for the faith.

The reason we have entire denominations that deny the deity of Christ, ordain homosexuals, and refuse to preach against sin is that Christians have forgotten the value of truth and the command to stand for it. And it didn't happen overnight. It happened as, over time, leaders downplayed truth for expediency, often under the stated intention of not offending a lost world.

This is a problem Francis Schaffer wrote about over thirty years ago: "Here is the great evangelical disaster—the failure of the evangelical world to stand for truth as truth. There is only one word for this—namely accommodation: the evangelical church has accommodated to the world spirit of the age."[1]

Schaffer's word for it is *accommodation*. Another word is *compromise*. As another author pointed out, "A great part of the evangelical community has transferred authority from *Sola Scriptura* to *Sola Cultura*."[2]

When churches become more concerned with how truth is received by unsaved people steeped in a godless culture than they are concerned with the truth itself, compromise is sure to follow. Compromise then leads to an accommodating theology that eventually leaves lost people the same as they were before they started—steeped in a godless culture without biblical truth. Vance Havner said it this way:

> Some Christians who once championed sound doctrine beat a retreat once in a while and from stratospheric heights announce that they do not 'stoop to controversy.' When a man contends for the faith in New Testament style he does not stoop! . . . Contending for the faith is not easy. It is not pleasant business. It has many perils. It is a thankless job. And it is highly unpopular in this age of moral fogs and spiritual twilights. It is a day of diplomats, not prophets. It is nicer to be an appeaser than an opposer. It is the day of Erasmus, not Luther; of Gamaliel, not Paul."[3]

---

1   Francis A. Schaffer, *The Great Evangelical Disaster* (Wheaton, IL: Crossway, 1984), 37.
2   Os Guinness, *Prophetic Untimeliness: A Challenge to the Idol of Relevance* (Grand Rapids, MI: Baker Books, 2005), 65.
3   Vance Havner, "The Forgotten Anathema," *Sword of the Lord*, January 7, 1955.

Indeed, we are living in a day of much dialogue and little standing. Truth matters. Especially when it's gone.

THE GRADUAL SLIPPAGE FROM TRUTH

Truth, of course, is not relative. Jesus *is* the truth: "Jesus saith unto him, I am the way, the truth, and the life: no man cometh unto the Father, but by me" (John 14:6). God's Word also is truth: "Thy word is true from the beginning: and every one of thy righteous judgments endureth for ever" (Psalm 119:160). "Sanctify them through thy truth: thy word is truth" (John 17:17). Furthermore, the local church is "the pillar and ground of the truth" (1 Timothy 3:15). It is our responsibility to "earnestly contend for the faith which was once delivered unto the saints" (Jude 3).

The pull away from truth, however, often begins with our associations. A younger pastor recently told me that it is the older generation who is forcing the younger generation to align with evangelical Calvinists and seeker movement leaders because older men are separating from them. While this has indeed been the case in some situations, I have discovered it is not always true. In fact, I'm finding that it is often the other way around. Those who are now identifying with the softer, non-denominational philosophy are moving away (separating) from their own parents, pastors, and mentors in their practice and, in some cases, their faith.

A slippage from the truth does not take place only among those who outright deny the veracity and authority of Scripture, but it also takes place by those who have allowed a series of compromises to pull them from their commitment to God's Word. It can take place even among Bible-believing Baptists who lose their focus on and willingness to firmly stand for the truth.

The gradual moving away from a position of strongly identifying with truth often follows leftward steps through the positions noted in the following spectrum.

PROPONENT   CONFORMITY   RELEVANCE   SEPARATION   ISOLATION

Let's take a closer look at each of these positions.

Isolation: Located on the far right of the diagram above is the *hyper separation* of those who refuse to fellowship with anyone who disagrees with them in any way—even when the person or group in question agrees fully in doctrine and 99 percent in ministry practice. This is where some of the ridiculous and petty separation has been practiced over issues such as slightly different dress or music standards, church architectural styles, whether or not a preacher wears a tie in the pulpit, and so on. Some churches and fellowships today have allowed past hurt or present insecurity to place them in isolation. Not only does this kind of separation not help those who practice it, but it is repulsive to those who yearn for a spirit of teamwork and have a desire to collectively reach their generation with the gospel.

Separation: In this book, I'll make a case for ecclesiastical separation practiced in a biblical way as being the proper position relative to truth. This separation from error is the only real foundation for unity. Those who obey the Bible commands in how they practice separation do so in a spirit of love with a commitment to contend for the faith.

Relevance: There is a very real sense in which relevance is needed in our articulation of truth and fits in with biblical separation on our continuum. But I use the term here to refer to a *focus* on relevance. Often those who are moving from a position of biblical separation do so while stretching relevance outside of its biblically-supported role. Relevance is a tool, not a target; and biblical landmarks are needed to keep relevance within the bounds of truth. When relevance becomes more important than the truth that should be driving it, compromise takes place.

Conformity: This is where someone crosses that blurry line between being relevant to today's culture and conforming to the spirit of the age.

Proponent: From conformity, the next step is becoming a proponent of a brand of grace and ministry that justifies carnal methods and yoking up with those who teach unbiblical doctrines. These proponents, as we will see later in this book, so misinterpret the doctrine of grace that they deny that there is a distinction between what is carnal and spiritual (1 Corinthians 3:1), much less a need to repent when we are carnal.

Where it concerns the truth or practices relative to the truth, compromise is always dangerous. The decay produced by compromise doesn't reveal itself immediately. Sometimes it takes years—perhaps even a full generation—before we can see the decayed fruit of compromise. This is why it is vital that we understand what God's Word says regarding standing for truth. When we follow the clear commands of Scripture, we do not have to wait for the erosion of time to know if we are on track.

THE CHURCH AS A MENTORING ENVIRONMENT FOR TRUTH

The church must not only hold the truth, but also declare it and model it. In Philippians 4:9, Paul wrote to the church he had planted at Philippi, "Those things, which ye have both learned, and received, and heard, and seen in me, do: and the God of peace shall be with you."

The world is constantly breaking down biblical distinctives and values. As Christians, then, we must teach and model these in our homes and churches with increasing clarity.

John Adams, second president of the United States, gave advice that I wish preachers would follow today:

> It is the duty of the clergy to accommodate their discourses to the times, to preach against such sins as are most prevalent, and recommend such virtues as are most wanted. For example, if exorbitant ambition and venality are predominant, ought they not to warn their hearers against these vices? If public spirit is much wanted, should they not inculcate this great virtue? If the rights and duties of Christian magistrates and subjects are disputed, should they not explain them, shew their nature, ends, limitations and restrictions, how much soever it may move the gall of Massachusettensis?[4]

In other words, pastors must not simply take a theoretical stand against sin in general, but we must directly address the issues of our day. I would add that we also must not theoretically promote a gospel-driven and Spirit-led life in general terms, but we must specifically instruct in and model the biblical teaching and living in areas that run counter to our culture.

Although not a comprehensive list by any means, here are a few areas, all mentioned by Paul to Titus, in which churches must specifically provide mentoring and modeling. These areas of instruction were needed in the first century, and they are still needed today.

Order—The stated reason Paul left Titus in Crete was to "set in order the things that are wanting" (Titus 1:5). This included ordaining pastors and setting church polity. As Baptists, we believe that the Bible

---

4   Charles Francis Adams, *The Works of John Adams, Second President of the United States*, Volume IV (Boston, MA: Charles C. Little and James Brown, 1851), 56.

is the sole authority in all matters of faith and practice (2 Timothy 3:16). Young Christians must see a commitment to biblical doctrine and New Testament church structure and function above any personal preferences or peripheral affiliations. They must see holiness in worship, doctrinally-sound singing, and Bible-filled, Christ-centered preaching. When the world tries to paint Christians as hateful or prudish, those within our churches need to understand that our convictions are rooted in Scripture and our loyalty is to Christ.

Integrity—The biblical requirement for a pastor or deacon to be "blameless" (1 Timothy 3:2, 10; Titus 1:6–7) is important in any culture. But in a culture that has become suspicious of anyone in a position of spiritual authority, it is especially vital. First Timothy 5:20 tells us, "Them that sin rebuke before all, that others also may fear." Bible-preaching churches cannot sweep criminal or moral failures of leaders under the carpet and expect continuing trust from a broken and hurting culture.

Masculinity and femininity—In a culture that pushes against the stereotyping of gender roles on one hand but then pushes for the crossing of gender distinctions on the other, the church must be the place where biblical, God-honoring gender is modeled in a way that points to our being made in the image of God and that embraces His divine order in the home and church.

The church should have ladies who model femininity and modesty. Titus 2:3–5 teaches that the local church is *especially* the place where this should take place. I'm not talking about lace and aprons, but about pure-hearted commitment to honor God's commands for modesty and to embrace God's plan for male leadership in the positions of pastor and husband.

The church should also model masculinity. Again, I'm not speaking of a macho man stereotype, and I'm certainly not advocating domineering leaders. But in a culture that degrades masculinity as toxic, young people and young Christians need to see what gracious, Spirit-filled masculinity looks like (Titus 2:2, 6–8). If the church doesn't model masculinity and femininity, who will?

Compassion—Our society is turning on itself, viciously attacking those who disagree with one's position as bigots or fearmongers. And ironically, all of this is done under the banner of greater inclusivity.

The church should be a place where there is an intense spirit of love for one another (1 Peter 1:22) and a Christ-filled compassion for the lost (Matthew 9:36). It should be the one place where a lost person who may be in complete opposition to every belief a church holds can know that they will be loved and that there will be people who care about them with a Christ-like love.

Our churches don't need less truth, and they certainly don't need to hide the truth behind entertainment-driven services. They need to declare the truth, and they need to cultivate a mentoring, discipling environment where the truth that stands in opposition to the world is presented and nurtured.

GRACE, TRUTH, AND LOVE

There are some Christians who assume that a discussion involving separation will necessarily be absent of love. They point to passages such as John 13:35 ("By this shall all men know that ye are my disciples, if ye have love one to another") and suggest that separation between Christians harms the testimony of the gospel and can only be incompatible with a spirit of love.

Indeed, Scripture does command us to have a loving spirit, and too often a stand for truth has been sullied by a disagreeable or pharisaical spirit. Yet, as surely as Scripture commands us to abound in love, it instructs us that our love is to be governed with knowledge and discernment: "And this I pray, that your love may abound more and more in knowledge and in all judgment; That ye may approve things that are excellent . . . " (Philippians 1:9–10).

The command to love is not the only command we have been given. Scripture also charges, "Buy the truth, and sell it not" (Proverbs 23:23). It tells us that "the church of the living God" is "the pillar and ground of the truth" (1 Timothy 3:15). We are commanded to love, and we are commanded to hold the truth. And we dare not do either at the expense of the other.

Biblical love is not tolerant of sin or false doctrine. In this day when "tolerance" is promoted as something of a Christian virtue, it is good for us to remember that Jesus praised the first-century church in Ephesus for their *intolerance* of false doctrine: "I know thy works, and thy labour, and thy patience, and how thou canst not bear them which are evil: and thou hast tried them which say they are apostles, and are not, and hast found them liars" (Revelation 2:2).

Let that sink in. Jesus *commended* intolerance. I fear that in all the dialogue of our day and the attitude of some to cozy up to those of differing views, a generation of Baptists are tolerating doctrine and practice they used to stand against.

A few verses after praising intolerance, Jesus rebuked the church in Pergamos for their tolerance: "But I have a few things against thee, because thou hast there them that hold the doctrine of Balaam, who taught Balac to cast a stumblingblock before the children of Israel, to eat things sacrificed unto idols, and to commit fornication. So hast thou also them that hold the doctrine of the Nicolaitans, which thing I hate. Repent; or else I will come unto thee quickly . . . " (Revelation 2:14–16).

A biblical Christian has an intense loving spirit for others but stands firmly for the truth. While I have for years stood against a spirit of threatening, arguing, and pharisaical pride in ministry, I stand very strongly with those who contend for the faith.

Almost forty years ago, Wayne Van Gelderen, Sr., who is now in Heaven, wrote an article challenging readers that to "contend for the faith" includes genuine engagement that can only be carried out through the power of the Holy Spirit.

> Now I can hear someone say—"But we need to contend without being contentious." If by that it is meant that we fight without landing a blow, or that we use paper swords, I reject it. We must contend vigorously! However, we need to be careful that we contend in the power of the Spirit and not the energy of the flesh. Carnality will confuse the message to the hearers. This does not mean that sharpness and force cannot be used. Spiritual contending does not mean weakness. Therefore, let us preach the truth in love—but let us be sure it is the truth![5]

Too many leaders desire the vocational benefits of ministry without being a partaker of the afflictions. They want to be a soldier without seeing combat. Yet, as Paul admonished Timothy, soldiers are partakers of the afflictions, not just the benefits, of the gospel: "Be not thou therefore ashamed of the testimony of our Lord, nor of me his prisoner: but be thou partaker of the afflictions of the gospel according to the power of God" (2 Timothy 1:8).

This book is a challenge to stand for the truth and to stand with others who do. But it is not a call to prideful contention. There is a difference

---

5 Wayne Van Gelderen Sr., *New Testament Association Newsletter* (Winter issue, January 1982), 1.

between contending and being contentious, and too often the spirit of the latter has hurt the former.

How can we contend for the faith without being contentious? The answer is simple, although not always easy: we speak the truth in love (Ephesians 4:15).

Too often, as Christians wade through topics such as we are about to embark on, there are angry words and hurt feelings on both sides—each accusing the other for both. A mark of spiritual maturity is not the ability to explain away truth; it is the ability to speak the truth in love. I trust this book will be so written—and received.

CHAPTER 2

THE DOCTRINE OF SEPARATION

I N THE FALL OF 2007, Beijing was preparing to host the following summer's Olympic games. While many people thought the Communist Chinese government would be less active in hindering the works of Christian ministry prior to the Olympics, the opposite proved to be true. The government became more restrictive toward unregistered churches—especially in Beijing.

I had the opportunity that fall to visit a number of American missionaries and Christian servants who serve in and around Beijing. Two of these men, both of whom work with underground churches, had their services disrupted by the police a few weeks prior to my visit.

I'll never forget one of the churches I visited. It was located in an upper story of a residential apartment building. There was no sign on the street to announce its presence or invite people in. Even in the hallway of the building, there was no indication that this apartment was any different from the other units.

Once inside, however, it was apparent you had walked into a house church. There was none of the usual household furniture, but there were rows of chairs, a pulpit in the front, and a keyboard off to the side. What most caught my attention, however, were the walls. Every outer wall of the apartment was lined with mattresses to absorb the sound and fend off the curiosity of reporting neighbors.

As the congregation gathered, quietly and in staggered groups of twos and threes—another safety precaution—I marveled at the courage of these Christians. I would soon be preaching through an interpreter, but even before the preaching, with no translator, I could sense my heart being knit to theirs. I sensed their love for Christ and commitment to worship Him under the direct threat of persecution. Even with a profound language barrier, there was a oneness, a sense of our shared love for the Lord. We worshipped Him together that morning—in different languages, but with a common bond.

I've had similar experiences (minus the mattresses and fear of the police) in South Korea, the Philippines, South Africa, Romania, Mexico, Costa Rica, Nicaragua, Finland, and many other countries. I can be with people whom I have never previously met and with whom I cannot easily converse and yet sense a unity between us.

What creates this bond? "One Lord, one faith, one baptism, One God and Father of all, who is above all, and through all, and in you all" (Ephesians 4:5–6). We are bound as brothers and sisters in Christ. Although we serve the Lord on different continents and worship in different languages, cultures, and settings, we share the same faith and the same Savior. Our doctrine—the body of beliefs we hold—binds us together.

Unity is a precious gift. It should be guarded carefully, and it should never be allowed to be undermined through personal, unresolved grievances. This is why Matthew 18 instructs us to go to our brother when there is something between us, and it is why Christ commands us to forgive one another. We should not allow personal offenses or petty differences to break Christian fellowship. In my opinion, there have been too many instances with Baptist leaders who have a carnal grievance against a brother, often rooted in pride and jealousy, and then assign a label of compromise in some form and call their disagreement "separation." That's not what we're talking about here.

But where there is not common doctrine, there cannot be biblical unity. As surely as shared doctrine unites, deviant doctrine divides. This is where those who suggest that unity is more essential than doctrine and that biblical separation is the enemy of unity are wrong. As previously noted, unity and separation are two sides of the same coin. Unity comes by common faith and practice, and separation is the result of incompatible faith and practice.

In future chapters, we'll examine the history of those who have separated for the sake of the truth. But first, we need a biblical framework for separation itself. What is it? And where is it taught in Scripture?

A BIBLICAL FRAMEWORK

The next several pages are a high-end overview—a basic theology—of biblical separation.[1]

---

1   For a fuller treatment of the biblical basis of separation that traces it all the way through Scripture, and even more throughout history than we will in this book, I suggest *Biblical Separation: The Struggle for a Pure Church,* 2nd ed. by Ernest Pickering (Arlington Heights, IL: Regular Baptist Press, 2008).

God is holy.

When Isaiah was given a glimpse into the throne room of Heaven, he was immediately overcome by the greatness of God's glory—so much so that the scene around the throne itself was the only aspect of Heaven that Isaiah recorded: "I saw also the Lord sitting upon a throne, high and lifted up, and his train filled the temple. Above it stood the seraphims: each one had six wings; with twain he covered his face, and with twain he covered his feet, and with twain he did fly. And one cried unto another, and said, Holy, holy, holy, is the LORD of hosts: the whole earth is full of his glory. And the posts of the door moved at the voice of him that cried, and the house was filled with smoke" (Isaiah 6:1–4).

"Holy, holy, holy." It's what the seraphim of Heaven cry out continually. It is a defining attribute of our God.

We tend to think of God's holiness as referring to His perfection, and it does. But holiness, as it pertains to God, refers to more than perfection. It refers to God's uniqueness—His transcendence and supremacy. God is above all and distinguished from all. "Who is like unto thee, O LORD, among the gods? who is like thee, glorious in holiness, fearful in praises, doing wonders?" (Exodus 15:11). "For thus saith the high and lofty One that inhabiteth eternity, whose name is Holy; I dwell in the high and holy place, with him also that is of a contrite and humble spirit, to revive the spirit of the humble, and to revive the heart of the contrite ones" (Isaiah 57:15).

In God, we see that perfect holiness and perfect love are never in conflict, as we think of it. Some people believe that Christians who live a separated lifestyle or churches who teach doctrinal separation are choosing holiness over love. In reality, holiness and love are *both* defining attributes of God, perfectly and consistently displayed in Christ: "For such an high priest became us, who is holy, harmless, undefiled, separate from sinners, and made higher than the heavens; Who needeth not daily, as those high priests, to offer up sacrifice, first for his own sins, and then for the people's: for this he did once, when he offered up himself" (Hebrews 7:26–27).

God calls His people to be holy.

When God calls His people to be holy, He is not putting them in a position to be unlike Himself. The prominent Greek word used throughout our New Testament referring to holiness is the word *hagios,* the root of which is found in words also translated *saint, separate,* and *sanctify.* It refers to something set apart—distinguished, sacred, or consecrated.

Because God is set apart, we must be as well. God Himself makes the connection: "For I am the Lord that bringeth you up out of the land of Egypt, to be your God: ye shall therefore be holy, for I am holy" (Leviticus 11:45). The New Testament quotes and repeats this instruction: "Because it is written, Be ye holy; for I am holy" (1 Peter 1:16).

To be holy unto God means to be separate from the world and all that the world represents—first in our doctrine and as an outflow in our lifestyle. The larger context of 1 Peter 1:16 makes this clear: "As obedient children, not fashioning yourselves according to the former lusts in your ignorance: But as he which hath called you is holy, so be ye holy in all manner of conversation; Because it is written, Be ye holy; for I am holy" (1 Peter 1:14–16).

Biblical separation is first a matter of the heart, and it is far larger than outward activities or appearances. In fact, one of the concerns that must be remembered when developing institutionally-enforced separation, such as may be used in a Christian school or college, is that students can develop the idea that separation from the world is about clothing styles, entertainment, and music. Of course these relate, but young people who see separation as *only* a list of rules, rather than a reflection of God's work from within, will eventually throw away the rule—either out of frustration or in hopes of discovering freedom to love God. Major Ian Thomas commented,

> There are countless thousands of young people who . . . have been evangelically house-trained. As they grow older and go off to a secular university or into the armed forces or into some other environment that detaches them from the evangelical mold to which they have been conformed, the results are inevitably disastrous. Confronted with the cold facts of life in a world of vastly different standards, they discover that they . . . simply did what made them acceptable to the particular religious group they adhered to at the time.[2]

Separation from "the world" is so much more than a list of dos or don'ts, because a biblical definition of "the world" is larger than what we do or how we look. It relates to values and philosophies, not just practices. We are called to have a deepening love for God that develops in us a hatred toward anything unholy or displeasing to Him. "Ye that love the Lord, hate evil" (Psalm 97:10).

Modern Christianity, however, has been hesitant—if not blatantly resistant—toward separation from error both ecclesiastically and personally. An abandoning of separation in doctrine was one of the most significant factors of the modern ecumenical movement, which began in the early 1900s with a goal to bring together all faiths, including Catholics, liberal Protestants, and Baptists, arguing that any differences

---

2   Major Ian Thomas, *The Indwelling Life of Christ: All of Him in All of Me* (New York: Multnomah, 2006), 145–146.

between them were smaller than the fact that they worshiped the same God. Likewise, a repudiation of separation was a driving force of the New Evangelical movement, which we'll look at in chapter 5. These have funneled into today's general prevailing disdain for the practice of separation.

Separation, however, is biblical, and we can trace it as a principle all the way through Scripture. At creation, God divided the light from the darkness. Throughout Genesis, we see the incompatibility of false worship and true worship. As God began the nation of Israel through Abraham, He gave circumcision as a symbol of the covenant He made with Abraham. This practice would mark the Israelites as God's special people. Later, through Moses, God gave specific laws regarding worship, relationships, and even appearance that would set the Israelites apart from surrounding nations. God wanted His people to be distinctly identified with Him.

Although we are no longer under the Mosaic Law, God still calls us to live as His special people: "But ye are a chosen generation, a royal priesthood, an holy nation, a peculiar people; that ye should shew forth the praises of him who hath called you out of darkness into his marvellous light" (1 Peter 2:9).

Separation is not division per se. It is a leaving of that which is false and a clinging to that which is true. It is embracing light and calling out darkness (Ephesians 5:7–12). It is refusing to attempt to mix oil and water—or to call them identical. Separation is, in its basic sense, living with a recognition that because God is holy—distinct from all else—He calls His people to be holy. Our identification with God requires our separation from that which stands in opposition to God.

The local church is called to be distinct in its doctrine.

The Greek word for *church* used in the New Testament is *ecclesia*, which means "a called out assembly."[3] The church was purchased by the blood of Jesus (Acts 20:28) and called out of the world as the people of God who are ambassadors for Christ.

The church is the pillar and the ground of the truth: "But if I tarry long, that thou mayest know how thou oughtest to behave thyself in the house of God, which is the church of the living God, the pillar and ground of the truth" (1 Timothy 3:15). It is to be the place where "the faith which was once delivered unto the saints" (Jude 3) is upheld and propagated. God has instructed the church to maintain its purity as individual local bodies directly accountable to Christ (Ephesians 5:23, Colossians 1:18). This requires separation from the sinful practices of the world (Ephesians 5:11) as well as separation from false doctrine (2 John 7–11).

The indication in the New Testament is that local assemblies, although they fellowshipped with one another (Colossians 1:4; 4:16), operated independently. The tendency of denominations, however, has been toward weakening or denying doctrine, rather than strengthening churches in it. Denominations today often reflect concerns of culture more than the concerns of God. They emphasize issues ranging from same-sex marriage to social justice. This tendency toward a less doctrinal emphasis has a direct bearing on the testimony of individual churches, because what happens in the denominational headquarters or seminaries has an effect on the associated local churches.

---

3   Strictly defining *ecclesia* as "called out assembly" relies more on etymology than every instance of use. It often just meant "assembly" or "those assembled for a purpose" as seen in Acts 19:32, 39, 41. When cross referenced with other Scriptures, however, it is clear that the biblical term as applied to the local church implies an assembly that is not of this world.

Actual apostasy has already taken place in many denominations. The results are both grieving and mind-boggling. Several years ago, the Claremont School of Theology, a United Methodist seminary located here in Southern California, received a $40 million gift designated and now being used to begin training programs for Muslim imams and Jewish rabbis. The school hopes to later add training for other religious clergy as well—such as Buddhists and Hindus.[4] I know that the United Methodist Church strayed many years ago from the fundamentals of the faith and has long been ecumenical in affiliations. But this news still surprised me. How can a group that professes to believe the Christian faith not see the impossibility of mixing Christianity, Islam, and Judaism? Of course, many celebrated this decision on the part of the school as a leap toward recognizing "religious diversity." But it is a leap that plunges truth downward rather than forward. I have read original sermons of John and Charles Wesley. I have visited their homes, church, and grave sites. I am confident this was not the intended direction for their affiliation of churches.

Purity in the local church is to be upheld both morally and doctrinally. Morally, this is done by church discipline, taught primarily in Matthew 18:15–18 (which emphasizes the goal of restoration) and 1 Corinthians 5:1–13 (which emphasizes the importance of practical purity in the church). As taught in the New Testament, church discipline is the responsibility of a local body, not of a denominational hierarchy. Doctrinally, maintaining purity is done by exposing and reproving error and false teachers. This protects against apostasy in a church, and, in practical terms, it can be called *separation*.

---

4   Larry Gordon, "Donation Will Allow Claremont School of Theology to Train Rabbis, Imams," *Los Angeles Times*, May 16, 2011, http://articles.latimes.com/2011/may/16/local/la-me-theology-20110516.

Separation in this sense is not based on a single, obscure text, but on repeated commands throughout the New Testament. Notice a few:

- In 2 John 7–11, God commands us to **have no fellowship with unbelief and not to entertain apostate teachers:** "For many deceivers are entered into the world, who confess not that Jesus Christ is come in the flesh. This is a deceiver and an antichrist. Look to yourselves, that we lose not those things which we have wrought, but that we receive a full reward. Whosoever transgresseth, and abideth not in the doctrine of Christ, hath not God. He that abideth in the doctrine of Christ, he hath both the Father and the Son. If there come any unto you, and bring not this doctrine, receive him not into your house, neither bid him God speed: For he that biddeth him God speed is partaker of his evil deeds." (See also 1 Timothy 1:18–20 and Titus 3:10.)

- In Romans 16:17, God commands us to **separate from those who teach contrary doctrine:** "Now I beseech you, brethren, mark them which cause divisions and offences contrary to the doctrine which ye have learned; and avoid them."

- In 2 Corinthians 6:14–18, He commands us to **not be yoked with unbelievers:** "Be ye not unequally yoked together with unbelievers: for what fellowship hath righteousness with unrighteousness? and what communion hath light with darkness? And what concord hath Christ with Belial? or what part hath he that believeth with an infidel? And what agreement hath the temple of God with idols? for ye are the temple of the living God; as God hath said, I will dwell in them, and walk in them; and I will be their God, and they shall be my people. Wherefore come out from among them, and be ye separate, saith the Lord, and touch not the unclean thing; and I will receive you, And will be a Father unto you, and ye shall be my sons and daughters, saith the Lord Almighty."

All of these commands are blatantly disobeyed by many in circles who reject the practice of ecclesiastical separation. I believe this is what has taken place in ecumenical groups such as the National Council of Churches (NCC) or World Council of Churches (WCC) where people of all types of religious affiliation and doctrine come together, as if such differences as salvation by faith alone, the inerrancy of the Scriptures, the virgin birth of Christ, and other clear biblical truths are inconsequential. "Doctrine divides, but service unites," is their watchword. In this they are correct, but I believe the division on lines of clear doctrinal truths is exactly what the verses above call for. Remaining true to Jesus Christ includes taking His commands for separation from error and apostasy seriously.

The local church is called to be distinct in its fellowship.

So, are the only reasons a church might separate from another church doctrinal in nature? Actually, no. Doctrine and fellowship, sometimes stated as "faith and practice," are linked in Scripture. Acts 2:42 describes early converts to Christ: "And they continued stedfastly in the apostles' *doctrine and fellowship,* and in breaking of bread, and in prayers."

While we are to love and pray for all Christians, doctrine and practice have always been guideposts for biblical Baptists. This is one of the reasons why most Baptist churches only accept transfer membership from someone from a church of "like faith and practice." Similarly, church covenants of Baptist churches have historically admonished members who move away to unite with a church of like faith and practice. Today, however, many Baptist pastors are uniting regularly with pastors of either unlike doctrine or practice.

We looked at New Testament commands for separation related to doctrine, but here are a few related to practice:

- In Ephesians 5:11, God commands us to **reprove error:** "And have no fellowship with the unfruitful works of darkness, but rather reprove them." Thus, we are not only to reprove false teachers as we saw earlier, but also unbiblical *practices* ("unfrutiful works of darkness"). In the context of this passage, the unfruitful works of darkness come from unsaved people. But whatever their source, we are to reprove error, not ignore it.

- In 1 Corinthians 5:11, God commands us to **not keep company with Christians living in open sin:** "But now I have written unto you not to keep company, if any man that is called a brother be a fornicator, or covetous, or an idolator, or a railer, or a drunkard, or an extortioner; with such an one no not to eat." Interestingly, the larger context of this passage specifies that we are talking specifically about *Christians* living in open sin, as opposed to unbelievers.

- In 2 Thessalonians 3:6, we are commanded to **withdraw from disobedient brothers:** "Now we command you, brethren, in the name of our Lord Jesus Christ, that ye withdraw yourselves from every brother that walketh disorderly, and not after the tradition which he received of us." The phrase *the tradition which he received of us* no doubt does refer to doctrine, but also to church polity and personal practice. In other words, if someone professes biblical doctrine, but their unbiblical lifestyle contradicts their profession, (in this case through laziness) they are walking "disorderly" and not "after the tradition" received by the apostles.

- In 2 Thessalonians 3:14, we are commanded to **have no company with belligerent brothers:** "And if any man obey not our word by this epistle, note that man, and have no company with him, that he may be ashamed." Thus, we are not to fellowship with someone who has made a deliberate refusal to submit to a clear scriptural teaching.

These commands are part of the reason why I choose not to preach with someone who is directly disobeying the New Testament commands regarding separation over doctrine. For instance, if someone is actively participating in the NCC or WCC, I believe they are walking in disobedience to God's Word. To then host that person in the pulpit of the church I pastor would create confusion among our members.

While some people refer to this reasoning as "second-degree separation," suggesting it goes beyond the scriptural command, I don't see it that way. I believe it is separation over the practical issues of obedience. Furthermore, I believe that it is a wise stewardship of the influence God has given me as a pastor.

When I was in Bible college, the most-often cited example of this kind of practical separation was if a Baptist should sit on a platform with a Roman Catholic priest at a meeting, such as in the Billy Graham crusades. (We'll look at the details of these crusades more thoroughly as we explore the history of New Evangelicalism.) But I'm not speaking here of old battles or instances of the 1950s. There are current issues that pastors today must consider. For example, a well-known author and pastor, Carey Nieuwhof, recently had a Catholic priest speak at his church. Neiuwhof then shared their commonalities on his blog. Speaking of the Catholic priest, he wrote, "Every denomination does things a bit different, but what unites us is far more important than what divides us."[5] I believe this position is disobedient to Scripture, and I would not invite Carey Nieuwhof to come preach for me for that reason. It is my conviction that

---

5   Carey Nieuwhof, "CNLP 118: A Roman Catholic Every Evangelical Leader Needs to Get to Know—A Conversation with Father James Mallon," *Carey Nieuwhof*, accessed October 10, 2019, https://careynieuwhof.com/episode118.

someone who endorses doctrine that is anti-biblical (such as Catholic doctrine) is not walking in obedience to God's Word, and I do not want to endorse that ecumenicalism.

Historically, a biblical fundamentalist held to sound doctrine and preached with those of similarly sound doctrine and practice. But there is a spirit of pragmatism very much alive today in which men, who verbally affirm the same doctrine and practice they once held, are distancing and differentiating themselves from those with whom they used to fellowship, while realigning themselves with those who believe and practice differently, sometimes even from entirely different faith traditions. In this change of affiliations, they are also changing Bible versions and ministry philosophies. The result is that they are building bridges back to cooperation with groups and philosophies that those in our past heritage who stood for truth walked away from. Getting new ideas and trying fresh methods is good, but walking over a bridge to ecclesiastical collaboration with those who don't share the same faith and doctrine is not good. I don't want to deviate from the faith intentionally by carnal choice or unintentionally by making weak alliances.

The argument for collaboration in these instances is often the common good of the gospel. As long as both parties believe in the inspiration of Scripture and salvation by faith, should doctrinal or practical differences matter? I believe they do, not only for the reasons I already shared, but also because of the reality of our influence.

INFLUENCE AND LEVELS OF COOPERATION

Even Christians who agree on the biblical commands for ecclesiastical separation over direct apostasy or conduct that is blatantly disobedient to Scripture sometimes disagree on other applications of separation.

For instance, how should we relate to those who may hold to the basic fundamentals of the faith but do not have the same doctrine, or to those who may have sound doctrine but closely associate with others who do not or who have seriously differing practice?

There are good, godly leaders who land on different places in answering these questions, and we need to acknowledge the roles of conscience and liberty here. But we also need to walk with wisdom, honesty, and discernment in how we apply the biblical commands to separate.

Wisdom allows us to avoid broad-brushing everyone who applies scriptural commands a little differently than we do (and this works in both directions—those who cooperate less than we would and those who cooperate more). Wisdom also allows us to apply these commands ourselves with discernment toward levels of cooperation and contexts of involvement.

Think of it this way: If you are in the army, you'll stand in the trenches next to anyone who shares your uniform—saved or unsaved. You just hope they're a good shot. If you're working against the opioid epidemic in your city, you might meet with people of like conviction, even if they are of different faiths, for the sake of your community. If you were at a funeral hosted by a church of another denomination, you might stand and pray.

In all of these cases, the context makes a difference. Inviting the pastor of the church you prayed with at the funeral to come preach in your church would provide a different type of endorsement of his doctrine than praying at the funeral.

When we discuss separation in these instances, I think it's important to point out that we are talking specifically here about sharing a platform or publicly recommending someone. There is a difference between a personal friendship and a ministry partnership. I can appreciate the ways in which God may be using someone who does not believe the same as I do without endorsing that person's doctrine to our church family by inviting him to come preach. So just because I "separate" from someone who loves the Lord and is preaching the gospel does not mean I publicly denounce this person as a heretic. It may just mean that I do not work as closely with them or choose to share a preaching platform.

The question for pastors and spiritual leaders becomes, with whom do we share platforms in ministry for the purpose of the proclamation of truth? Another angle from which to look at it might be, what amount of cooperation could or should we share with another Christian leader?

These questions have both philosophical and practical aspects that may come into play. For instance, inviting someone to serve on my staff is a closer partnership than happening to be invited to preach at the same conference. Quoting from someone's book may be a simple point of academic honesty, while inviting that author to preach at my church is more of an endorsement. Some of these considerations may be unique to the stewardship of pastoral influence. As a pastor, I do not want to do anything that would cause confusion in the hearts of our church family over doctrinal differences or ministry convictions.

Again, godly leaders draw the lines in varied places, and there have been differences in how independent Baptists practice ecclesiastical separation. Dr. Lee Roberson and Dr. Tom Malone differed slightly on who they had preach on their platforms (one had conservative Southern Baptists, and the other did not), yet they were friends. Both, however, told me they were cautious to discern the doctrine and philosophical direction of a guest speaker.

I have no desire to police other churches or ministries. But I do have a desire to remain true to the doctrines of God's Word, to obey the explicit commands of Scripture regarding separation, to take a distinctive position strongly holding to sound doctrine, to proactively guard the flock, and to personally "contend for the faith which was once delivered unto the saints" (Jude 3).

IDENTIFY WITH TRUTH

When it comes to questions related to cooperation, we should ask ourselves, "Will this cooperation strengthen my influence for truth? Will it identify me more closely or less closely with the doctrines and practices I preach?"

As pastors, our closest church fellowship and preaching engagements should be based on the closest doctrinal unity. When I became pastor of Lancaster Baptist Church, I received the doctrinal statement of the church and felt it would be my responsibility to uphold the doctrine and only bring in guest preachers who held to the same doctrine.

I recently preached at a conference in Michigan where the new pastor had succeeded R. B. Ouellette, who has been my friend and who pastored at that church for over forty years. The new pastor, J. D. Howell, is a millennial with some new methods and ideas for ministry. But as he opened the conference, he explained that he wants to be faithful to the historic doctrine and practice of the church. In a day when books are written and conferences held on how to transition a church to different philosophy and often different doctrine, I found Pastor Howell's comments refreshing.

I remember as a young man hearing the phrase, "Over the course of your ministry, you will either change your convictions or your friends." If in keeping your convictions, you must lose a friend, it is better to hold to the truth.

In the past few decades, I have observed leaders moving away from their primary fellowship being with conservative Baptists of like faith and practice into a broader religious world. As is the case with much we'll look at in this book, this is nothing new. It was happening when I was in my twenties, as men with whom I attended college were dropping the name Baptist, changing church government, and creating new identities and new levels of cooperation for their churches. The issues today are similar. Men who were raised in strong Baptist churches are moving away from points of doctrinal and ministry distinction as they seek new alliances, worship styles, Bible versions, and identities.

Some of these men I know personally. I love them dearly. We have preached together and labored together. I have spoken to many of them about my concerns for the direction of Christianity in these last days and for Baptists in particular. These men are not my enemies; they are my brothers. We do not always agree and may not fellowship as closely as we once did, but we must pray for one another and be open to kind dialogue.

While independent Baptist pastors cherish freedom and liberty, we must also use our liberty responsibly. Part of that responsibility includes considering how the alliances we make today will impact the churches our children attend tomorrow.

I have in my files a letter from Curtis Hutson, a contender of the faith from the generation before me, which he wrote me during an acute battle with cancer and just a few months before he went to be with the Lord. One paragraph reads, "I challenge you to take your place in the long line of independent, fundamental Baptists who have stood for separation and soulwinning (and I speak now especially of ecclesiastical separation) and to hold that banner high until Jesus comes or God calls you Home." I treasure this letter, its admonition, and the relationship I had with Dr. Hutson. I appreciate the stand that he and a long line of people before him have taken as they have been willing to identify with the truth—even when it meant separating from error. Although I've had my share of detractors who, for whatever reasons, have tried to place me on a slippery slope, I intend to take a firm stand on the Word of God and to abide by the biblical principles that further the propagation of the truth.

In our next chapter, we'll trace a brief history of those who have stood for the faith and for the doctrine of separation. Their commitment to keep the faith gives us courage to press on in full commitment to Christ and His truth.

CHAPTER 3

A HISTORY OF BIBLICAL FUNDAMENTALISM

EVERY FEW MONTHS, I STAND in front of several dozen adults who are new to Lancaster Baptist Church and teach what we call our Core class. Often, the room is filled with newly-saved, first-generation Christians with plenty of great questions.

I share the history of Lancaster Baptist Church—how God miraculously revived a congregation of twelve adults and has grown our church into a family of over eight thousand members today. I teach through our doctrinal statement and Baptist distinctives. And I share with them why our church is a Baptist church, as well as what it means to be independent of a denomination and to stand for the fundamentals of the faith.

It's important to me that our church family not only understand our doctrine, but that we know our history, including the victories God has given our church family. Our shared history is part of what forms our vision for the future and perspective for the present.

Likewise, I believe it is important that independent Baptist leaders know their history as well. What was the fundamental movement all about? Why did the early fundamentalists separate from the modernists? Why have there been significant points of separation among Baptists? Does any of it still matter today?

In my observation, those who have become hesitant to practice or are critical toward ecclesiastical separation have known little about the history of separatists and, if an independent Baptist, have heard a skewed perspective on the points of separation that developed the independent Baptist movement. Many also have not understood the original premises of the New Evangelical movement and why fundamentalists (including, but not limited to, independent Baptists) did not want to be associated with it. For those reasons, I will attempt in these next two chapters to give some historical perspective on fundamentalism, the independent Baptist movement, and New Evangelicalism. I'll do my best in these chapters to give a historical overview while landing here and there to point out significant highlights.

To fully understand fundamentalism as a movement, you have to look at a larger picture than the setting of the 1800s in which it first took shape, just as to understand American history, you have to look at the larger picture of world history. Although the landmark dates of American history—1776 when fifty-six men signed the Declaration of Independence or 1620 when the Pilgrims landed or 1492 when Columbus discovered the New World—are relatively recent, our history traces back much further. In fact, it's impossible to properly understand the events that shaped our nation without understanding the significant events that predated them in Europe. Similarly, fundamentalism—as a movement—has a relatively short history, officially tracing back to only the 1800s. (I realize that *fundamentalism* is an often-despised and easily-misunderstood word. You may prefer *biblicist* or *orthodox,* which is fine as well. I'm using it in this chapter from a historic perspective and in the pure definition of the word—adhering to the basic tenets of the faith.)[1]

Recent as it may be, however, the emergence of the fundamental movement relates to truths held by Christians and local churches since the first century. As biblicists, we don't see ourselves as independent of history or as beginning later than when Jesus Himself established the New Testament church. The doctrine and beliefs we hold were not discovered in the late nineteenth century as a reaction to modernism and further defined in the 1950s as a reaction to New Evangelicalism. We simply believe, seek to practice, and commit to stand for first-century Christianity.

I WILL BUILD MY CHURCH

The local New Testament church was not man's idea or creation. It was in the plan of God from eternity past, kept shrouded in mystery through the Old Testament (Ephesians 3:9), and finally revealed in the New Testament (Colossians 1:26–27).

---

1. In modern vernacular, the words *fundamentalism* or *fundamentalists* are sometimes misunderstood as referring to fringe or extreme religious positions—such as Islamic fanatics or organizations like Westboro Baptist Church. For this reason, I don't use the term when speaking with the media or non-Christians who are unfamiliar with the actual definition and historic meaning behind it. As discussed in this chapter, fundamentalism as a movement refers historically to Christians in the 1800s who refused to allow the basic tenants—fundamentals—of their faith be swept away by liberalism. When explaining the term to young Christians or new church members, I point out that just as a coach in basketball camp will teach the fundamentals of the sport, so we can define ourselves as fundamentalists because we believe the fundamentals—the basic truths—of the Bible and Christianity.

Even the apostles couldn't have comprehended the fullness of Jesus' declaration when He said, "Upon this rock I will build my church; and the gates of hell shall not prevail against it" (Matthew 16:18). And yet, two thousand years later, neither time nor persecution has weakened this promise. In fact, the only way to explain the past two thousand years of history as it relates to the church is that it has been providentially and supernaturally preserved.

One of the clear messages from the book of Acts is that the evangelism and church planting efforts accomplished by local churches was possible because of the unity and fellowship within and among churches. From the members of the church in Jerusalem having all things common (Acts 2:44) to the church of Antioch sending missionaries (Acts 13:3) to new church plants supporting missionaries as they continued to carry the gospel to regions beyond (Philippians 4:15–16), these were people unified around the gospel message.

Of course, even in the first century there were detractors and false teachers. Their efforts were met by the apostles with sharp rebuke (Galatians 1:6–9) and commands to believers to separate from them (Romans 16:17, Titus 3:10). From the early days of the local church, separation from that which was false was vital to preserving the purity of the church. Even as our doctrine is not new, neither is our practice of separation. It can be traced through the centuries as a thread connecting churches committed to purity under the headship of Christ.

Moving forward from the pages of the New Testament into the second and third centuries, we come to one of the most significant challenges of church history in the forming of a state church, which became the Roman Catholic Church. Prior to this time, Bible-believing Christians continued to experience severe persecution all throughout the Roman Empire. Then, the emperor Constantine "converted" to Christianity through his alleged vision of a cross in the sky before an unlikely military victory. He followed this event by making Christianity legal in the empire. A little over a decade later, Constantine called the Council of Nicaea (325 A. D.), setting the precedent that the emperor could play a significant role in church affairs. In 390, Theodosius I followed by making Christianity the official religion of the Roman Empire.

While some churches (perhaps genuinely believing in Constantine's conversion and Theodosius' good intentions, or perhaps weary from three hundred years of unrelenting persecution) joined this new state religion, others did not, believing that only Christ could be the head of the church (Colossians 1:18). There were other doctrinal issues, too, that came in mixing the church and the state, including relabeling old paganism to fit Christian terminology. Perceptive, Bible-believing Christians repudiated the state church and continued to function as local, New Testament churches, often in secret. Ultimately, the development of a unified state church empowered Roman Catholic leaders to demand emperors to persecute those who refused this unbiblical church. (Those persecuted included our Baptist forefathers.) The Church of Rome quickly compromised, distorted the gospel, and wedded herself to the state in such a way that pragmatism and power trumped truth and purity.

But just because some compromised truth does not mean New Testament churches did not still exist. Indeed, a closer look throughout Europe reveals pockets of persecuted but courageous bodies of believers who held to the basic truths of New Testament Christianity and refused to join themselves with an organization so corrupted as the Roman Catholic Church.

From the Montanists in the second century to the Novatians in the third century to the Donatists in the fourth and the Albigenses throughout the Middle Ages, we find believers who courageously stood for truth and actively proclaimed the Bible. Although some of these groups, or at least some factions of them, misinterpreted and misunderstood significant Bible doctrines, they were stout in their allegiance to Christ and in their operation as called out assemblies of Christians.[2]

The history of these groups is hard to trace, and there isn't a large amount of written history published during their era because they were persecuted and martyred and their records burned. But the history of these faithful Christians is a history of standing for Christ, even when it meant risking all by refusing to be joined to the Roman Catholic Church and her political protections.

Sometimes I contrast the weak doctrinal stands of churches today with the stone caves I visited in the Piedmont valley of Italy where the Waldensians not only held services in secret, but also trained young men as preachers of the gospel. For these Bible college students, their lives were something like a race against martyrdom. All of them knew they were likely to be killed for spreading the gospel, so they desired to share it as effectively as possible until then. I'm grateful they did.

But what if they hadn't? What if they had taken the view of so many in our culture today that the end justifies the means? That as long as a preacher has a desire to see people saved and people are making professions of faith in Christ, whatever he is doing must be fine?

After all, the Waldensians could have blended in. They could have justified remaining in the Catholic church and performing its sacraments only as a way to infiltrate the general population and perhaps even the priests with the message of the gospel. They could have rationalized that

---

2   For more history on these groups, see *A Glorious Church* by Mike Gass (Lancaster, CA: Striving Together Publications, 2009). For history on these groups specifically in regards to the principle of separation, see *Biblical Separation: The Struggle for a Pure Church*, 2nd ed. by Ernest Pickering (Arlington Heights, IL: Regular Baptist Press, 2008).

sharing the gospel from a position of persecution was not only difficult, but also unattractive to potential new converts.

But they didn't. They hid and studied and preached and gave their lives . . . and they still saw converts come to Christ. In fact, their boldness and witness was so effective that the Roman Church tried in vain to stomp them out. The "Massacre of Piedmont" in 1655—one of the most horrific and satanically-gruesome persecutions of history—was four hundred years after Peter Waldo began preaching. Ecclesiastical separation is not the death knell people today would have us to believe.

I would go so far as to say that the willingness of these baptistic groups (the Waldensians and others) to show their allegiance to Christ by practicing separation from the Roman Church is what God used to preserve His churches through the dark ages—fulfilling His promise that even the gates of Hell could not prevail against it.

SEPARATION DURING THE REFORMATION

Following the spiritual darkness of the mid-centuries, God used the Reformers to break the political power of the Roman Catholic Church, bring widespread use of God's Word and hearing of the gospel, and lead Europe out of the Dark Ages. Of course, a Baptist perspective on the Reformation is more mixed than a Protestant perspective. Where Protestants hail the Reformation for its theological breakthroughs, Baptists look back on it with wry gratitude. In the long term, it broke the stranglehold of the Catholic church on Europe and did much to spread the gospel across the continent. Furthermore, it was led by courageous men who were willing to risk their lives for the doctrines of salvation by grace alone and the church's loyalty to Scripture.

Yet, the facts of history stand that even the Reformers persecuted Baptists (and other non-conformist groups). I've stood by the River Lammat in Switzerland where Felix Manz was drowned for preaching believer's baptism and baptizing others. Reformer Ulrich Zwingli (who had actually led Manz to Christ) was largely responsible for Manz' execution.[3] But it wasn't just Manz. One author wrote that there were more Anabaptist martyrs after the Reformation than there were Christians who died in the early persecutions of Rome.[4]

How the Reformers—the very men who risked their lives for truth—could turn and persecute others who had already been standing for the same truths but differed on other points of theology and practice (such as infant baptism) is a mystery I've never been able to wrap my mind around. Yes, the Reformers were flawed men and often held flawed theology. Nevertheless, God did use the Reformation in significant ways spiritually and historically.

I mention the persecution here, however, simply to again note that New Testament churches with Baptist beliefs predated Protestants and were separatists in the biblical sense long before Protestant groups were in the political sense. Historically, we existed before, during, and after the Reformation, as even early Baptist persecutors testified in the two quotes below:

> Cardinal Hosius, President of the Council of Trent, A. D. 1550:
> "If the truth of religion were to be judged of by the readiness and cheerfulness which a man of any sect shows in suffering, then the

---

3　For a chapter-length biography of Felix Manz, see *Outsiders: 15 Leaders Who Followed Christ and Changed the World* (Lancaster, CA: Striving Together Publications, 2019).

4　This statement is included in *Rescuing the Gospel: The Story and Significance of the Reformation* by Erwin Lutzer (Grand Rapids, MI: Baker Books, 2016), 158. The book is a remarkable history of the Reformation with two full chapters devoted to Anabaptists and the strange persecution they endured at the hands of some of the Reformers.

opinion and persuasion of no sect can be truer and surer than that of Anabaptists (Baptists) since there have been none, for these twelve hundred years past, that have been more generally punished, or that have more cheerfully and steadfastly undergone, and even offered themselves to, the most cruel sorts of punishments, than these people."

Zwingli, co-laborer of Calvin: "The institution of Anabaptism is no novelty, but for thirteen hundred years has caused great disturbance in the church, and has acquired such a strength, that the attempt in this age to contend with it appeared futile for a time."[5]

Charles Spurgeon also pointed to Baptists as existing long before the Reformation and remaining separated from state churches.

We believe that the Baptists are the original Christians. We did not commence our existence at the reformation, we were reformers before Luther or Calvin were born; we never came from the Church of Rome, for we were never in it, but we have an unbroken line up to the apostles themselves. We have always existed from the very days of Christ, and our principles, sometimes veiled and forgotten, like a river which may travel underground for a little season, have always had honest and holy adherents. Persecuted alike by Romanists and Protestants of almost every sect, yet there has never existed a Government holding Baptist principles which persecuted others; nor I believe any body of Baptists ever held it to be right to put the consciences of others under the control of man. We have ever been ready to suffer, as our martyrologies will prove, but we are not ready to accept any help from the State, to prostitute the purity of the Bride of Christ to any alliance with the government, and we will

5   C. A. Jenkens, *What Made Me a Baptist* (Watertown, WI: Roger Williams Heritage Archives, 1901), 12–13.

never make the Church, although the Queen, the despot over the consciences of men.[6]

There are those today who, in a spirit of pragmatism, feel that if they drop the name *Baptist* and loosen up on their identity, they will better be able to reach people with the gospel. I disagree. In part, this is because the name ties us to the Baptist forefathers—specifically the Anabaptists— who courageously stood for truth and were martyred for preaching the doctrines of salvation by faith and the local church comprised of saved, baptized believers. I've stood at too many of the sites of their martyrdom to have any interest in backing away from a position that strongly identifies our church with the biblical convictions for which they stood. But the other reason is that while a church that drops the name Baptist might attract a few people (and, for that matter, it might turn away or fail to attract a few people), I believe that it ultimately hurts that church as a whole because it weakens the church's doctrinal clarity and identity.[7] Our name gives clarity and states a commitment to Bible doctrine and a courageous heritage. As a pastor, I would rather educate those who, for whatever reason, may be leery of the name than avoid its benefits.

Some people suggest that the Reformation and its doctrinal differences with the Catholic church is over. They believe that all who claim the name of Christ should put the past behind and enjoy unity today. But as

---

6   Charles Spurgeon, *The New Park Street and Metropolitan Tabernacle Pulpit,* Volume 7 (London: Passmore and Alabaster, 1862), 225.

7   Some raise a question on this point regarding churches such as the one Charles Spurgeon pastored (the New Park Street Chapel, later renamed the Metropolitan Tabernacle) which did not include the name Baptist. The difference is that often nineteenth-century churches (such as Spurgeon's) didn't have Baptist in their name to begin with. My concern is over those who are dropping the name. Another point of the historical context regarding Spurgeon is that, even without the name Baptist, the church strongly and publicly identified as a Baptist church, and Spurgeon never shied away from identifying himself as a Baptist. (See, for example, the lengthy quote by Spurgeon on the previous page.) So not including Baptist in the church name was not an effort to distance themselves from clear identification.

Erwin Lutzer so clearly articulated in his helpful book on the history of the Reformation, *Rescuing the Gospel,* it's not that straightforward.

> With the new openness between evangelicals and Catholics, we shouldn't be surprised that some evangelicals are turning to the Catholic Church both for instruction on practices, such as contemplative prayer, and for joint ventures in worship and mission. Evangelical pastors and institutions are forging bonds with Catholics to demonstrate the unity of the church and to explore common ground between them. This sounds like such a wonderful idea that many evangelicals wonder why this isn't done more often in our churches, Bible colleges, and seminaries. . . . After all, Jesus said unity was to be a powerful sign of His presence among His people.[8]

He details some of the perceived points of doctrinal agreement, explaining that they agree in carefully-worded sidestepping of issues only, and then continues:

> We welcome the good will that has developed between evangelicals and Catholics and are glad that we can cooperate on such issues as opposition to same-sex marriage and abortion, along with fighting for freedom of religion and other such matters. But when it comes to the central issue of the gospel, the gap between us is just as wide as ever.[9]

Ecumenical compromises don't strengthen the side which holds the truth. They weaken the position of truth.

---

8   Erwin W. Lutzer, *Rescuing the Gospel: The Story and Significance of the Reformation* (Grand Rapids, MI: Baker Books, 2016), 187–188.

9   Lutzer, *Rescuing the Gospel: The Story and Significance of the Reformation,* 190.

THE BIRTH OF FUNDAMENTALISM

Crossing the Atlantic from Europe into the New World colonies, many are the tales of churches wrestling through the issues of separation— primarily regarding separation from the state churches—Anglican, Lutheran, or Presbyterian. Secular historians see these turbulent times as a political struggle. But in truth, it was a struggle for freedom of conscience—a struggle to have Christ as the head of the church and to follow pure doctrine.

In fact, it is the biblical distinctives of individual soul liberty and separation of church and state that have historically defined Baptists and their forefathers as advocates for freedom of conscience and religion. Even here in the United States, it was Baptists, including men such as Obadiah Holmes and Roger Williams, who led the way both in suffering for their convictions and insisting on freedom for all. It was the influence of Baptists that brought about the religious freedom we know in America today through the First Amendment to the United States Constitution.

In the early years of the United States, even before the War for Independence, God gave us the Great Awakening (1730–1755). After the war, He gave us the Second Great Awakening (1790–1840). Through both of these periods of revival, which were both precipitated by great spiritual drought, God developed a nation in which there were widespread conversions and, even among people who were not saved, a widespread familiarity with core Christian values.

Then came the Civil War, which had a decidedly counter effect on the revival fires of the Second Great Awakening. After the Civil War, German Rationalism and Modernism began to take root in American society—first in her academic institutions and then in her pulpits. Just before the Civil War, Charles Darwin published *The Origin of the Species* (1859). Through this book and the influence of unbelieving theologians, liberalism—the outright denial of biblical revelation—began taking hold in denominations and churches across America. Christians struggled to reconcile secularistic science and faith. Leading pastors shifted their preaching from literal, practical, specific declarations of Scripture to idealistic, social, allegorical speeches. A landslide of liberalism infiltrated all denominations, even the Baptist conventions in both the northern and southern states.

It was in response to this liberalism that modern fundamentalism was born, and God gave America the Third Great Awakening (1855-1900) largely led by such men as D. L. Moody and R. A. Torrey. Those who rose up to defend the faith were called fundamentalists and were openly ridiculed by pastors and academic leaders who called themselves liberals. In 1909, A. C. Dixon and R. A. Torrey began to compile and publish what would become a twelve-volume set titled *The Fundamentals: A Testimony to the Truth.* These articles, featuring the work of many authors, underscored five nonnegotiable tenets of the Christian faith. Collectively, they came to be known as the "Five Points of Fundamentalism." They are as follows:

1. The inerrancy of Scripture
2. The virgin birth of Christ
3. The substitutional atonement of Christ
4. The bodily resurrection and future second coming of Christ
5. The authenticity of the biblical miracles

These were never meant to be a full statement of faith (conservatives in every denomination had a much larger body of nonnegotiable convictions), but it was a written stand against all that liberalism represented.

By and large, the strongest fundamentalists were Presbyterians, Methodists, and Baptists. These were not necessarily connected across denominations, except in a shared allegiance to standing against liberalism. Primarily, fundamentalists in each denomination or convention fought their own battles against liberal leadership in their seminaries and churches.[10] In the next chapter, we'll zero in on Baptist fundamentalists and see how the commitment to biblical doctrine among Baptists during this era gave rise to the independent Baptist movement.

---

10   For a history of Fundamentalism, see *In Pursuit of Purity: American Fundamentalism since 1850* by David O. Beal (Greenville, SC: Unusual Publications, 1986).

CHAPTER 4

RECENT BAPTIST HISTORY

Among Baptists at the time of the Fundamentalist-Modernist controversies, there were two large conventions—the Northern Baptist Convention and the Southern Baptist Convention. There were fundamentalists in both conventions, but it was the northern convention that first fell to liberalism, thus it was from the northern convention that fundamental churches first began pulling out.

We'll look briefly at how this played out in both the north and the south. But before we get there, I want to highlight the three primary reasons why the leaders and churches that pulled out of the conventions believed they must break these affiliations:

- The conventions collected churches' missions monies and used it to support missionaries who didn't believe the gospel or the fundamentals of the faith.

- The conventions corrupted the young minds of students in their seminaries—young people who had been mentored and trained by fundamental pastors—teaching them straight, unadulterated liberalism.
- The conventions elected men to leadership positions within the conventions who literally and blatantly disbelieved the Bible and the gospel.

In short, they left because they believed in the principle of separation and did not want to participate in the spread of error.

THE NORTHERN BAPTIST CONVENTION

The Northern Baptist Convention was first organized in 1814 under the name "General Missionary Convention of the Baptist Denomination in the United States of America for Foreign Missions." Its purpose, as indicated in its name, was to collaborate in the support of missionaries, specifically Adoniram and Ann Judson. Eventually it came to be known as the Triennial Convention (because they met every three years) or the American Baptist Convention, then the Northern Baptist Convention, and now it goes by American Baptist Churches USA.

Sadly, as modernism began sweeping across our nation in the early 1900s, it infiltrated the Northern Baptist Convention. Prominent pastors and seminary leaders, supported by wealthy donors, began preaching liberalism and, in place of the gospel, preaching a social gospel. In 1922, liberal pastor Harry Emerson Fosdick clearly demonstrated this decisive shift to liberalism with his watershed message titled, "Shall the Fundamentalists Win?"

Seeing a hardened determination toward liberalism, fundamentalists began pulling out of the Northern Baptist Convention en masse by the 1930s. These were the beginning days of what is now called the Independent Fundamental Baptist Movement. These men were already *fundamentalists*, but they saw no way to retain doctrinal integrity while associated with a convention that repudiated the core doctrines of Scripture, thus they became *independent* as well.

One of the early leaders of the independent Baptist movement in the north was Pastor Robert Ketcham, who led other newly-independent churches in organizing the Baptist Bible Union, which became the General Association of Regular Baptist Churches (GARBC).[1] The GARBC is still in existence today and operates the Regular Baptist Press publishing.

Later, another large group of churches that pulled out of the Northern Baptist Convention formed the Conservative Baptist Convention. (B. Myron Cedarholm was an early general director of the CBC.) In contrast to the GARBC, the CBC retained much of the denominational-type structure of the NBC, especially in relation to its giving model and in what churches supported its missionaries and training institutions. Over the first two decades of its existence, the CBC became increasingly less conservative, with fundamental churches in the convention facing familiar concerns about how their support was being used to support liberal (and later, New Evangelical) missionaries as well as professors in the CBC-related colleges and seminaries.[2]

Eventually, after some years of raising concerns and pleading for a return to doctrinal clarity and purity to no avail, Cedarholm resigned as general director and helped form the Fundamentalist Fellowship, which became the Fundamental Baptist Fellowship (FBF). From the beginning, the FBF structured itself differently from a denomination in that it operated as a

---

1   Kevin Bauder and Robert Delnay, *One in Hope and Doctrine* (Arlington Heights, IL: Regular Baptist Books, 2014), 185–218.
2   Richard Clearwaters, who was the first president of the CBC, details these concerns and their progression in his book *The Great Conservative Baptist Compromise* (Minneapolis, MN: Central Seminary, 1963).

nonbinding, voluntary fellowship for pastors and other individuals, but not churches. In this way, churches were truly autonomous in operation and in the missionaries and training institutions they supported.

Some look at these divisions and blame the fundamentalists for a lack of unity and charity. After all, it was the fundamentalists who kept breaking off and forming new groups. In each of these instances of separation, however, the new groups that formed did so out of a commitment to uphold biblical doctrine and further the spread of the gospel around the world. Furthermore, when you look at the wide-ranging doctrinal and practical positions of the American Baptist Churches USA (formerly the Northern Baptist Convention), I believe the fundamentalists are vindicated. Today, American Baptist churches perform same-sex marriages, ordain women, and avoid imposing a clear doctrinal position on their affiliated churches. Theologically and morally, they are liberal.

THE SOUTHERN BAPTIST CONVENTION

The original formation of the Southern Baptist Convention is an example of a split that was neither biblical nor honorable. It was just before the Civil War (1845), and the Baptist churches in the South pulled out of the Northern Baptist Convention over the issue of slavery. (The southern churches were opposed to abolition. The convention has since renounced and apologized for this position.)[3]

Remarkably, however, as the NBC drifted doctrinally in the early 1900s, the SBC held its ground a couple decades longer. But eventually,

---

3   "Resolution on Racial Reconciliation on the 150th Anniversary of the Southern Baptist Convention," *Southern Baptist Convention*, 1995, http://www.sbc.net/resolutions/899/resolution-on-racial-reconciliation-on-the-150th-anniversary-of-the-southern-baptist-convention.

the SBC followed the NBC in liberalism and apostasy. By the 1940s, many pastors in the south were also pulling out of their convention.

While most of the newly-formed groups in the north (such as the CBC) had, as noted above, called for membership from the churches that wished to be part of the group, the groups that formed in the South started out as loose fellowships of pastors for the cause of missions and education with no binding obligation of membership or giving to a central fund. One of these was the Southwide Baptist Fellowship, which is still in existence today.

The largest group that formed was the World Baptist Fellowship (WBF). This group traces its origins to one of the most well-known fundamentalist Baptist pastors of the 1900s—J. Frank Norris. Norris' bold preaching and unapologetic stand for fundamental doctrine and practice attracted hundreds of Baptist pastors who were experiencing unrest in their spirit over the doctrinal compromises within the Southern Baptist Convention. Through leaving the convention himself and through his preaching and leadership skills, Norris blazed the trail toward independence.

Over time, the World Baptist Fellowship struggled with mounting logistical and financial tensions. In a 1950 pastors' meeting, these tensions came to a head, and G. B. Vick (a previous WBF president) launched the Bible Baptist Fellowship (BBF), which still exists today. (I was trained for ministry in a BBF school.)

Of course, not every church that left a convention became part of another fellowship of churches. And some associated with multiple fellowships. Today, many independent Baptist churches, while not officially identified with a particular group such as BBF or GARBC, still enjoy fellowship with other churches that are. This is the position of the church I pastor.

There have been other groups that have formed as well. And there have been some splits that were not over doctrine but, with the vantage point of time, over petty disagreements. For the sake of time, I won't detail each. Suffice it to say, however, that none of these minor divisions have been what started the independent Baptist movement, and none of these have been what defined the movement to many of us who choose to be independent Baptists.

There are weaknesses in any group. And those who criticize ecclesiastical separation or the independent Baptist movement often point to some of the lesser points of separation as proof that separatists are mean-spirited and independent Baptists were formed over divisive personalities. The first claim is not necessarily true, and the second is false.

So why did these early independent Baptists—in both the north and the south—choose to pull out of the conventions rather than simply keep their own churches fundamental in doctrine and stay in? After all, there still were men who loved the Lord and believed biblical truth staying in the conventions. Why not try, like them, to be a voice for purity within?

We already saw the three primary reasons related to missions support, training the next generation, and doctrinal purity. But there was more than that. Being independent Baptist meant that they had freedom to serve as the Lord led their conscience. In fact, the very idea of those who left the conventions was that *independent* would simply be an adjective. It was never meant to be an identifying label in the sense that all who were independent would hold to the same preferences. Rather, it was just a way of saying, "I hold Baptist doctrine, but I am not associated with liberal groups who claim the Baptist label but are in groups that refuse to take a true stand for its doctrine."

Those who left faced difficult and courageous decisions. In many cases, pastors who pulled out lost their churches, or at least their church buildings and property which had been purchased by the conventions. They also lost their salaries, pensions, and financial security. Sometimes they lost dear friends. They moved into storefronts and began again preaching the gospel and laboring with Christ to build His church.

I was privileged to know many of the first-generation leaders of the independent Baptist movement. Men such as John R. Rice, B. R. Lakin, G. B. Vick, Monroe Parker, and B. Myron Cedarholm stayed in our home when I was a boy. A few, including Lee Roberson, Tom Malone, and Don Sisk preached in our church after I became a pastor. Most of them are now in Heaven.

I know these men weren't perfect and that the independent Baptist movement isn't without its flaws. I highlighted ten all-too-common imbalances in my book *The Road Ahead*. But it grieves me today when men who never knew these leaders, after reading books or articles written by people with decidedly opposing convictions on separation and who have painted caricatures of their faults, do not appreciate their sacrifices or courage.

I saw them weep for lost souls. I heard them pray for God's power. I listened to them talk about biblical convictions. They were men of God who loved Christ and His church, studied God's Word, and courageously stood for truth. Even my Southern Baptist friends who remember these men respected their conviction for doctrine and soulwinning.

WHAT ABOUT THE SOUTHERN BAPTIST CONVENTION TODAY?

In one of the most surprising doctrinal comebacks of church history, the Southern Baptist Convention made a conservative resurgence in the 1980s. Because of this, I am sometimes asked by young independent Baptists, including students in my college class, what my thoughts are on joining the SBC now.

The conservative resurgence officially began in 1979 when Adrian Rogers was elected as the president of the SBC. Through strategic planning and execution over a ten-year period, conservatives were able to appoint other conservatives to the various boards and committees within the national organization. From this position, they were able to oust the liberal presidents and professors from the seminaries.

I respect men like W. A. Criswell, Adrian Rogers, R. G. Lee (I have a Bible in my office signed by him after I heard him preach his famous sermon "Payday Someday" as a boy), Jerry Vines, and others for their fight for fundamental doctrine in the SBC. In Jerry Vines' autobiography, *Vines: My Life and Ministry,* he describes the challenges of those years. (Interestingly, Vines not only stood for the inerrancy of Scripture and fought liberalism; he also stood against liquor, including social drinking, and rock music in services. I thought it was significant that, like many independent Baptist leaders, he recognized that a commitment to truth includes both doctrine and personal holiness.)

Vines served as the president of the SBC for two consecutive terms—from 1988–1989. He not only worked to bring back a doctrinal resurgence, but he also worked to bring back an emphasis on reaching lost people with the gospel. In his autobiography, he mentions the impact Lee Roberson (who pulled out of the SBC) made on his life in the area of soulwinning, and he describes how he determined that would be the focus of his presidency in the SBC.

> I soon announced the theme for my presidency would be personal soul winning. I would call our denomination to renew its commitment to one of the activities that had made it great. And, should I be reelected,

my second year emphasis would be building great soul-winning churches. I recommitted myself to being a faithful witness for the Lord. I purchased a little red notebook and recorded the date, name, and some brief explanation of people I won to the Lord that year.[4]

Now at eighty-two years old, Dr. Vines shares the concerns of many for the future of the group he once served. In fact, I have several Southern Baptist friends and acquaintances who are on the conservative edge of that group. They are solid in doctrine, preach a "whosoever will" gospel, and care about holiness in lifestyle. I am thankful for these men and for the victories they have seen in doctrinal truth in their convention as well as souls saved in the churches they pastored.

But as I see it, a new era in the SBC has dawned. It is one that is much more concerned with social justice than the gospel and espouses worldly lifestyles including openly drinking alcohol.[5] In fact, it is telling to me that the independent Baptists I know who are trending toward the SBC do not seem to be modeling their ministries after R. G. Lee or Jerry Vines with a goal toward holy living, conservative worship, and abstinence from alcohol. They are following flashier, edgier leaders who may be seeing conversions, but are setting a direction for ministry that is creating a church more in step with the world than with the cross of Christ. I fear where this direction will lead the next generation.

Even though I appreciate the conviction of the remaining conservative men in the SBC, I would not want to be a part of it for a few reasons:

---

4   Jerry Vines, *Vines: My Life and Ministry* (Nashville: B&H Publishing Group, 2014), chap. 14, Kindle.

5   I believe in complete abstinence from alcohol for several reasons, including God's specific commands against drunkenness, the word *wine* in Scripture being used to refer to both alcoholic and non-alcoholic beverages, and, particularly in the context of this book, the principle of not causing another to stumble. For a more thorough treatment of these thoughts, see the booklet I wrote titled *Should a Christian Drink Alcohol?* (Striving Together Publications, 2014).

First, while it is true that the SBC is the only large convention or denomination to make a conservative resurgence from liberalism, it is not true that there is no liberalism within the convention. The resurgence was executed, in essence, through strategic outmaneuvering of the liberals, but there was no convention-wide repentance of liberalism and turn back to biblical truth. In fact, the trend back to a majority of conservatives in positions of leadership and withdrawing from the ecumenical Baptist World Alliance was gradual and took a full twenty-five years (1979–2004). There are still SBC churches today that lean liberally, and the SBC has no real way to ensure otherwise. (Of course, an independent Baptist has no way to ensure that those who choose that label are biblical, but the difference is that the independent Baptist has no convention affiliation tying them to such churches.)

The SBC is structured so that not only is there a national convention (in which the conservative resurgence took place), but there are also state conventions which govern themselves independently of the national convention. The state conventions have not all made the conservative resurgence as the national convention. Some states (particularly Texas and Virginia)[6] have openly challenged the conservative resurgence of the national board, and their state conventions have retained dual affiliation with the SBC as well as with more "moderate" cooperative programs and boards.[7] While I am grateful for the renewed emphasis of biblical truth in

---

6   "SBC Conflict Splits Virginia Baptists—Moderates and Conservatives of the Southern Baptist Convention," *Christian Century,* November 20, 1996.

7   Both states, of course, have local churches that are conservative in doctrine. But the funds given to these state conventions are sent to the national SBC as well as to the Baptist General Convention of Texas (BGCT) and the Baptist General Association of Virginia (BGAV). Both of these identities have the doctrinal and ecumenical issues the SBC had before the conservative resurgence. For instance, the openly-liberal Baylor University is affiliated with, supported by, and partially governed by the BGCT. The BGAV partners in support with the Cooperative Baptist Fellowship (CBF), a theologically-moderate group formed in backlash to the SBC conservative resurgence.

the SBC over the past three decades, I am concerned with the emphasis of supporting committee men who are broadly affiliated and further support at state levels churches or organizations not holding to the faith.

Another reason I personally could not join the SBC is because of the broad doctrinal tent it shares with people espousing Reformed theology—both regarding soteriology and ecclesiology.[8] A 2012 LifeWay Research survey found that 30 percent of SBC pastors consider their churches to be "theologically Reformed or Calvinist."[9] I believe this is a significant issue, especially as it relates to cooperatives in missions. I very strongly hold to a "whosoever will" gospel and am grieved that such a large group within the SBC is moving to Reformed doctrine.[10]

The resurgence of Calvinism in recent decades has come through loud and strong. Sometimes this is in the form of classical Calvinism, but there is a growing number of leaders who identify themselves as New Calvinists or Neo Calvinists. Collin Hansen, a Calvinist himself, describes this in his book *Young, Restless, Reformed.* Making a case in his prologue for the tremendous interest in Calvinism among younger leaders, he writes:

> If anything, in my limited sphere I saw a return to traditional Reformed theology. My friends read John Piper's book *Desiring*

---

8   I have benefited greatly from my study of the Reformers and thank God for their courage. I have friends who are Reformed. But I cannot subscribe to a system of theology that places God in the position of predetermining to send some people to Hell, based on His choice, not theirs. I recommend the book *Whosoever Will: A Biblical-Theological Critique of Five-Point Calvinism* by David L. Allen and Steve W. Lemke (Nashville, TN: B&H Academic, 2010) for understanding Calvinism from a theological perspective.

9   "SBC Pastors Polled on Calvinism and Its Effect," *LifeWay Research*, June 19, 2012, https://lifewayresearch.com/2012/06/19/sbcpastors-polled-on-calvinism-and-its-effect.

10   Separation over Reformed doctrine is nothing new. For instance, in the 1800s there was a separation of the Regular and the Particular Baptists, largely over this very issue. (Particular Baptists believed that the atonement was only for a particular few.) Once again, this is not about making a statement of censure, but about supporting those who share a church's doctrinal statement.

God and learned from Wayne Grudem's *Systematic Theology.* They wanted to study at the Southern Baptist Theological Seminary....I started thinking about leading seminaries in the United States and noticed a number of Calvinists in leadership positions. I considered millions of books sold by Piper and his yearly appearances at the popular Passion conference.[11]

Another reason I would not join the SBC is that I am concerned by its general direction that seems to be moving toward replacing personal evangelism with a gospel of social justice. As I write, there is significant controversy within the SBC on a national level regarding issues related to social justice, woman pastors, "woke" awareness, intersectionality, and Critical Race Theory. This drift has become obvious even to those within the convention with more conservative leanings. In recent months, a group of SBC pastors formed the Conservative Baptist Network, hoping to strengthen the conservative position. Their initial press release read, in part, as follows:

A significant number of pastors and laymen, motivated by a passionate desire to keep the Southern Baptist Convention anchored to the inerrancy and sufficiency of God's Word, have formed the Conservative Baptist Network. The Network is the product of a grassroots movement that developed organically in the hearts and minds of devoted Southern Baptists who have become concerned about the current direction and perceived future of the convention.

A significant number of Southern Baptists are concerned about the apparent emphasis on social justice, Critical Race Theory, Intersectionality, and the redefining of biblical gender roles. Many

---

11   Collin Hansen, *Young Restless, Reformed: A Journalist's Journey with the New Calvinists* (Wheaton, IL: Crossway Books, 2008), 11–12.

fear that these issues have received more attention than evangelism and spiritual renewal . . . .[12]

I appreciate the heart of these men to call out these issues. Sadly, it seems they are in a minority position today.

Finally, I am not interested in joining the SBC because I am not comfortable with its missions cooperative. Historically, financial support to the central missions cooperative was one of the very reasons independent Baptists pulled out of the convention. It was convictions regarding the biblical teaching of separation that motivated first-generation independent Baptists to refuse to give to or receive funds from a convention because it became a tie to a ministry philosophy they could not support. This is one reason it concerns me when independent Baptist church planters today set aside their independent heritage to raise money, including soliciting support from non-independent Baptist mission organizations.

A FIRST-HAND ACCOUNT

I mentioned earlier that many of my mentors had been in the SBC and pulled out. As time goes on, many of those men have gone on to be with the Lord, and few pastors just starting out in ministry have gotten to hear a first-hand account of why they left and what their perspective is today. So I'd like to give you that inside glimpse from one of the men who left the SBC when it was still liberal—Dr. Don Sisk.

---

12   "Pastors, Laymen Launch Conservative Baptist Network Press Release," *Conservative Baptist Network*, February 14, 2020, https://conservativebaptistnetwork.com/press-release/.

I recently asked Dr. Sisk to describe his story and his reasons. He first gave three reasons for having left: the SBC missions program, the liberal doctrine, and ecclesiastical identification.

Dr. Sisk described what it was like as a pastor in rural Kentucky in the 1960s to learn that only a small percent of the money their church gave to the SBC cooperative missions fund was actually going to missions work and the remaining money was going to organizations such as the World Baptist Fellowship or the World Counsel of Churches—non-fundamental and ecumenical organizations their church would never have supported.

Then Dr. Sisk told about visiting Louisville seminary as a prospective missions student (he was called into missions while serving as a pastor) and hearing lectures that undermined the very deity of Christ and miracles of the Bible. Later he learned that there were actually faculty members who taught that the first eleven chapters of Genesis were a myth. He began reading what the professors were writing and learned several were committed liberals. He discovered faculty members were going to Germany to study and converting to German Rationalism, which they brought back to SBC seminaries and actively taught. Obviously, the fundamentalists in the convention who were working to clean up these issues were also concerned.

But my favorite part of hearing Dr. Sisk describe why he left the SBC was the final reason, which he called the "positive reason." He went to a Bible conference and heard independent Baptist preachers and not only sensed their commitment to Christ and a literal belief in Scripture, but also their great burden for souls. He said to himself, "That's what I believe and who I want to be. These people are more who I am than the leaders in the SBC." Dr. Sisk said his heart was challenged to hear of soulwinning in the independent Baptist churches. He also mentioned the spirit of camaraderie that he felt among the pastors at this conference. (I believe this spirit is needed again in the independent Baptist movement.) When he learned of the independent Baptist model of missions giving through local churches, the idea further resonated in his heart.

Dr. Sisk left the SBC in 1963 and never looked back. After leaving, he and his wife Virginia served as missionaries in Japan, planting two churches, one of which is the largest independent Baptist church in Japan today. Eventually, Dr. Sisk became the General Director for Baptist International Missions, Inc. (BIMI) and then the chairman of the missions department here at West Coast Baptist College. Probably no one in our generation has done more for the cause of missions than Don Sisk. To this day, in his eighties, he continues to preach internationally as well as across our nation, bringing the needs of millions of people still waiting on the gospel before local church congregations.

After Dr. Sisk described why he left the SBC, I asked him specifically, "Given the conservative resurgence of the SBC, if you were in now, would you leave?" His answer was immediate: "Yes." And it may surprise you that the three reasons he gave were virtually the same as the reasons he left: missions, doctrine, and identification.

First, Dr. Sisk said he is still not comfortable with the cooperative program of the SBC because it supports a variety of SBC programs that may not be connected with the biblical convictions of convention pastors. He also explained that a small percentage of the SBC cooperative mission program goes to actual on-the-field, gospel-preaching missions work. According to the SBC website, "The Cooperative Program is Southern Baptists' unified plan of giving through which cooperating Southern Baptist churches give a percentage of their undesignated receipts in support of their respective state convention and the Southern Baptist Convention missions and ministries."[13] Additionally, the cooperative program is used to finance the North American Mission Board (namb.net), International Mission Board (imb.org), the Ethics & Religious Liberty Commission (ERLC), and the six Southern Baptist seminaries in America.[14] (Many have concerns with the ERLC leaning toward a social justice agenda. In fact, there have been a number of SBC churches withholding funds from the cooperative program over such concerns.)[15]

The doctrinal reason Dr. Sisk gave why he would still not be part of the SBC today is that, while he is thankful for the conservative resurgence that reaffirms basic fundamentals of the faith, Reformed theology is taught in the SBC seminaries. Personally, he would not want to be in a convention of that nature, and practically, he would not want to encourage young people to train for the ministry where they would likely become Reformed.

Finally, Dr. Sisk explained that he is grieved to see many SBC churches rebranding themselves without the name Baptist. Although they may technically remain a Baptist church, maintaining their membership in the SBC and including Baptist somewhere in their doctrinal statement or church documents, they have renamed their churches without the identification. Whatever you may believe about using the name Baptist (which I strongly believe in because it provides doctrinal clarity and honors our heritage), you can understand why someone would be concerned about being a member of a group that claims to be Baptist

---

13　"The Cooperative Program," *Southern Baptist Convention,* accessed November 13, 2019, http://www.sbc.net/cp.

14　"Five Facts about the Cooperative Program," *Ethics and Religious Liberty Commission,* November 6, 2014, https://erlc.com/resource-library/articles/5-facts-about-the-cooperative-program.

15　https://baptistandreflector.org/ripple-effect-withholding-cooperative-program-giving/

but shies away from the name. Dr. Sisk mentioned that, as part of this rebranding, many of the SBC churches he knows of practice no or little ecclesiastical or personal separation.

Like me, Dr. Sisk has friends who are Southern Baptist. We, as well as every gracious, godly independent Baptist pastor we know, appreciate the work of those within the SBC who are preaching the gospel and leading people to Christ. But one does not have to join a group simply because he appreciates the good within that group. I still believe that being independent allows for greater liberty of conscience and stronger forward momentum in missions and soulwinning.

CHAPTER 5

A HISTORY OF
NEW EVANGELICALISM

IN MAY OF 1847, ARCHAEOLOGIST Clermont-Ganneau made a discovery which he described as a "rich contribution to the . . . epigraphy of Palestine."[1] He had uncovered a horizontal slab inscribed in Greek and Hebrew that reads "limit of Gezer." Months later, he discovered a second similarly inscribed stone approximately 1,700 yards due northwest of the first.[2] For archeologists, these stones confirmed the location and dimension of one of the "Cities of Refuge" described in Joshua 21:21. For Bible students, they are a silent testimony to the "ancient landmarks" described in Scripture.

Landmarks in Bible days were not only demarcations of city limits; they were also used as property markers. The Mosaic Law expressly

---

1   "Letters from M. Clermont-Ganneau," *Palestine Exploration Fund Quarterly Statement for* 1874. (N.p.: Oxford University, n.d.), 276.
2   Ibid, 280.

prohibited moving or overstepping the boundaries marked by such a stone (Deuteronomy 19:14, 27:17), and Proverbs 23:10 and 22:28 reiterate those commands. To move a landmark was to steal property from another.

Moving landmarks was particularly egregious in Hebrew society because the land was handed down from generation to generation as an inheritance from one's fathers. It is for this reason that various commentaries on Proverbs 22:28 suggest that the command regarding physical landmarks can be applied to moral and doctrinal landmarks as well.[3] The ancient landmarks—those things that have been believed and held dear by Christians through the centuries—do not need to be relocated or revised. They need to be defended.

Today, however, we hear "reasoned" appeals to re-examine our beliefs and consider how we might make them more palatable to the unsaved world. While we should be aware of the realties around us and be appropriate in our witness, we must not live under the delusion that we can adjust our convictions to appease the world. The landmarks of our faith are founded in Scripture, and it is the task of our generation to defend those truths, not change them or strip them down to a less robust form.

When we look at the history of New Evangelicalism, however, we find that it was birthed in a reaction to the dogmatism and separation of the fundamentalists.

Although *New Evangelical* is now an old label, the philosophy behind it continues today, which is why it is important to understand its history and the assumptions in which it was rooted. Christians who believe in the command to contend for the faith can apply the lessons learned from New Evangelicalism to today's labels.

---

3   John Gill, H. D. M. Spence *(Pulpit Commentary)*, Adam Clarke, A. C. Gaebelein, Matthew Henry, and Joseph S. Exell *(Biblical Illustrator)* all suggest this application.

THE BEGINNING OF THE NEW EVANGELICAL MOVEMENT

If you didn't catch it from the previous chapters, some of the most defining points of church history in America have revolved around wars. The Great Awakening preceded the War for Independence, and the war seems to have ended it. In God's grace, the Second Great Awakening followed and then a third, but World War 1—a tragic, satanically-devised onslaught of destruction—distracted from this work of God's grace. And the liberalism that was already creeping in began to take over.

Something similar happened after World War II. War-weary Christians, tired of both the global conflict and the fundamentalist-modernist battles, were offered promises of unity if they would only embrace a series of compromises.

New Evangelicalism (a term adherents chose for themselves) was not the opposite of fundamentalism in *doctrine*. It primarily differed in *practice*. Basically, it was a call to truce with the liberals—a suggestion that fundamentalists could believe what they did without separating from those who denied it, so long as the deniers called themselves Christians.

Of course, New Evangelicals didn't phrase it in those words. They couched much of their call to lay down arms of contending for the faith in verbiage relating to attitude, calling leaders to take a softer, more reasonable attitude toward Bible-deniers. Harold Ockenga, one of the earliest leaders of the movement said it this way: "The evangelical and the fundamentalist could sign the same creed," but "an evangelical must be distinguished from a fundamentalist in areas of intellectual and ecclesiastical attitude."[4] The hope was that if the fundamentalists would

---

4   Harold J. Ockenga, "Resurgent Evangelical Leadership," *Christianity Today* (October 10, 1960), 12–13.

become more intellectual and less dogmatic, they could draw the liberals back to the truth. The New Evangelicals felt they could build a bridge to reach the liberals and bring them back over to the truth. Unfortunately, a bridge can go both directions, and it did.

The coming out moment of the New Evangelical movement was when Harold Ockenga delivered a speech at Fuller Theological Seminary in Pasadena, California, in which he outlined the basis of Neo-Evangelicalism. He described this moment nearly three decades later:

> Neo-evangelicalism was born in 1948 in connection with a convocation address which I gave in the Civic Auditorium in Pasadena. While reaffirming the theological view of fundamentalism, this address repudiated its ecclesiology and its social theory. The ringing call for a repudiation of separatism and the summons to social involvement received a hearty response from many Evangelicals. . . . It differed from fundamentalism in its repudiation of separatism and its determination to engage itself in the theological dialogue of the day. It had a new emphasis upon the application of the gospel to the sociological, political, and economic areas of life.[5]

You can see from Ockenga's statement that New Evangelicalism was, from its conception, a reaction to fundamentalism and to separation. Many Southern Baptists and independent Baptists today are reacting similarly. They are not merely rejecting personalities like R. G. Lee or Tom Malone, but also the premillennial, pretribulation, soulwinning doctrine. Also, you can see its insistence on social justice and involvement as well as its repudiation of separation in order to have greater dialogue with the broader religious world.

---

5   Harold Ockenga, foreword to *The Battle for the Bible,* by Harold Lindsell (Grand Rapids, MI: Zondervan Publishing House, 1976), 11.

When I teach my Practical Theology class at West Coast Baptist College about the history of New Evangelicalism, I explain the basic difference between fundamentalism, liberalism, and the middle ground of New Evangelicalism this way:

- Fundamentalism is the truth declared.
- Liberalism is the truth denied.
- New Evangelicalism is the truth compromised.

Fundamentalists have long been known for their dedication to hold fast and their concern to set forth the great truths of God's Word. We saw in chapter 3 the historic meaning of the word *fundamentalist*—one who firmly stands on and contends for the basic tenets of the Christian faith.

Liberals outright deny the truth—selling it wholesale. Some deny the reality of miracles, the inspiration of the Bible, or the scientific accuracy of God's Word; others deny the reality of truth itself or say that truth cannot be known.

New Evangelicals made it clear in the beginning that they wouldn't deny truth—they believed it. But they didn't believe ecclesiastical separation from others who did deny truth was loving; thus they yoked up with those who denied truth. In fact, as we will see in a moment, this openness to liberals is part of the self-chosen criteria to New Evangelicals for their label. (Incidentally, what sets fundamentalists apart from the broader label of *evangelical* is the principle of separation and a decisive stand for truth. New Evangelicals took this a step further in that they repudiated taking a dogmatic stand for truth, and they specifically disassociated from fundamentalists.) This lenient position to error, however, compromises truth. Unfortunately, the New Evangelical reluctance to take a stand with and for truth has opened their position to denial of truth and to its exclusive claims.

Once again, we see these earmarks in current trends. A recent president of Fuller Theological Seminary, Richard Mouw, followed in Ockenga's footsteps in calling for greater dialogue, this time with the Mormons. In a 2013 interview, in which he was responding to evangelical backlash after he stood on the platform of the Mormon Tabernacle in Salt Lake City and apologized to the Mormons for Christians misunderstanding them, he defended his comments. While stating he still has theological differences with Mormons, he definitively said he does not believe they are a religious cult and may not be as different as we think. In his interview, he stated, "Mormonism is to Christianity very similar to what Christianity is to Judaism. That is, there's continuity and discontinuity. In the early days, Christianity was seen as a cult to the Jews. Jews no longer think of us as a cult or a sect. And I think we owe the same thing to our Mormon friends."[6]

In the book *Adventures in Evangelical Civility: A Lifelong Quest for Common Ground,* a memoir which Mouw wrote a few years after the interview mentioned above, he acknowledged,

> I still worry about unintended consequences of what I have advocated
> for over the past several decades [finding human commonness rather
> than theological differences], and the worry nags me as I reflect back.
> While I am convinced that each aspect of my quest for commonness
> was meant to achieve something worthwhile, the net effect of all
> those efforts could very well encourage some bad tendencies.[7]

The "net effect" of New Evangelical compromises may not be what its advocates want, but neither is it surprising. It is the consequence of refusing to contend for the faith once delivered unto the saints.

---

6   Calvin University, "An Evangelical Apology to Mormons," YouTube video, 26:51, posted by "Calvin University," February 21, 2013, https://youtu.be/nflH3U6_4K8.

7   Richard Mouw, *Adventures in Evangelical Civility: A Lifelong Quest for Common Ground* (2016), Brazos Press, Introduction, kindle edition.

THE PREMISES OF THE NEW EVANGELICAL MOVEMENT

Less than a decade after Ockenga announced the beginning of the New Evangelical movement, an article in the March 1956 edition of *Christian Life* magazine promoting the New Evangelical movement presented an eight-fold premise for it.[8] The bold points given here are from the article; the notes after each are my explanation or refutation.

1. **A friendly attitude toward science**—This meant a friendliness toward or acceptance of evolutionary theories. New Evangelicalism has always placed a premium on intellectualism, and from early on, this was a premium at the expense of direct revelation.

2. **A re-evaluation of the work of the Holy Spirit**—This would open the door to acceptance of Charismatic doctrine.

3. **A move away from dispensationalism**—This was noted specifically by Okenga in his speech at Fuller Theological Seminary. Reformed eschatology versus dispensational eschatology tends to be a consistent theological difference between separatists and non-separatists.

4. **A more tolerant attitude toward varying views on eschatology**—More than a difference between a pretribulation or posttribulation rapture, this relates to the difference between a literal or allegorical reading of passages on prophecy. It's not so much a call for leniency on a slightly different interpretation for a single passage, so much as a move away from a historical, contextual, literal approach to Scripture.

5. **Renewed emphasis on scholarship**—This was not a call for fundamentalists to be more scholarly. It was, like point one above,

---

8   "Is Evangelical Theology Changing?," *Christian Life*, March 1956, 16–19.

a call for fundamentalists to accept the opinions of "experts," even when they disagreed with Scripture, including in areas such as textual criticism of Scripture itself.

6.   **Renewed emphasis on social responsibility**—This is something you'll see often in groups pulling away from a separatist position. There is a concern that separation means isolation and that Christians are abandoning their community and social responsibilities toward the poor and needy. The result of this emphasis is usually a focus on social gospel missions and a lessening of personal soulwinning and evangelism.

7.   **Re-examination of biblical inspiration**—Is the Bible itself really inspired? Is it just the overall thoughts and ideas, or the specific words? This deals not only with the doctrine of inspiration but also preservation.

8.   **Willingness to dialogue with liberal theologians**—This one also relates to the intellectual credibility issue. It's not a "willingness to share the gospel with liberal theologians," but a willingness to have open-ended discussions about clear theological matters. It directly counters the biblical commands for rejecting false teachers and exposing apostasy.

I see several of these trends on the rise in the ministry philosophy of some independent Baptists today. And this concerns me.

Understand that Ockenga as well as other prominent leaders in the New Evangelical movement were fundamental in their own beliefs, at least as far as ascribing to the "five fundamentals" goes.[9] They outright

---

9   As referenced in chapter 3, the "Five Points of Fundamentalism" outlined by A. C. Dixon and R. A. Torrey in their 1909 publication were as follows: 1) The inerrancy of Scripture. 2) The virgin birth of Christ. 3) The substitutional atonement of Christ. 4) The bodily resurrection and future second coming of Christ. 5) The authenticity of the biblical miracles. Okenga and other New Evangelicals believed all of these.

rejected the label *fundamentalist* as pejorative, but these men were not liberals. In fact, Billy Graham was one of the early embracers of New Evangelicalism, and he was not a liberal by any stretch of the word.

THE BRIDGES OF A NON-SEPARATIST POSITION

There's much to admire and appreciate about Billy Graham. He preached the gospel for many decades. He was kind. He was never involved in a moral or financial scandal. And he was a bold voice for moral integrity in a decaying culture. (I am also grateful for the stand his son Franklin Graham takes against the moral decay in the United States today.) Billy Graham went to Heaven in 2018, while I was working on this book. Immediately after his death, as a tribute to his long and fruitful ministry, thousands of people shared how they trusted Christ while hearing him preach. I personally know many who were saved through the ministry of Billy Graham, and I am grateful for every salvation.

But Graham also collaborated with leaders of all faiths, including inviting Catholics and pastors of churches in openly liberal denominations, to help sponsor his evangelistic rallies. And when I say "sponsor," I don't mean "accept donations from," but literally to sit on the platform, lead in prayer, and be assigned some of the follow-up contacts of those who made decisions for Christ. A member of our church walked out of a planning meeting for the Los Angeles crusade when the Catholic priests were introduced. A man who is now on our staff told me that he went to help counsel those who came forward to receive Christ at the Cleveland crusade in 1972. He described the instructions the counselors were given: "If you meet a Roman Catholic, direct him to the Catholic counselors; if Charismatic to the Charismatic counselors," and so forth.

Fundamental leaders were concerned about Graham's collaboration with leaders of other faiths. Many reached out to him about it. Evangelist John R. Rice wrote to Graham about this shared sponsorship and received a response defending Graham's position:

> Graham went on to inform Rice that he did not see much importance in ecclesiastical separation from liberals (as he defined them) in his campaigns. He wrote, "It does not seem to me that the line should be drawn too firmly in sponsorship. Where the lines must be drawn is in the public presentation of the gospel and the personnel of the team associated with the evangelist. That is where I draw absolutely strict lines." This adherence to a true, biblical gospel would turn out to be a major defense by Graham and his supporters against Fundamentalists in days to come. The argument was that if the gospel was preached in all its power in an evangelistic campaign, sponsorship and cooperation were irrelevant. Perhaps even the liberal could get saved through the right message.[10]

I'm sympathetic to the idea of a liberal hearing the gospel and being saved. I don't believe that endorsing the liberal by allowing him to help sponsor a meeting helps anyone, especially new or weak Christians.

The April 2018 issue of *Christianity Today*, dedicated to Graham's memory, gives more examples of the kinds of bridges Graham formed. One paragraph under the heading "Building the New Evangelicalism" is telling:

> Graham did more than evangelize. By the mid-1950s he shared the vision of Harold Ockenga, Carl F. H. Henry, and others for a new evangelicalism that would shed the skin of fundamentalist

---

10   This exchange is included in a not-yet-published book by John R. Himes titled *John R. Rice and Billy Graham* which draws from the *JRR Papers*, letter from Graham to Rice, January 10, 1956.

extremism. It would still be conservative at its theological core but would broaden beyond dispensationalism. It would take a softer line on evolution, engage mainstream scholarship, and take "a definite liberal approach to social problems." Most importantly, it would deploy the parachurch to spread evangelical faith among mainline Protestants and then draw them into evangelical networks.[11]

So while on the one hand, I appreciate the fact that Billy Graham preached the gospel and there are many aspects of the man himself that I admire and respect, I also believe he confused people in significant ways through his alliances.

I state now, as I did earlier, that I'm grateful for every person saved and for every preacher of the gospel. What we're talking about here then is not labeling men as "false teachers." It is recognizing the practical applications to the specific commands of Scripture we looked at in chapter 2 regarding having nothing to do with false teachers, such as 2 John 7–11 and Romans 16:17. From a standpoint of stewarding God-given leadership influence, to join on a preaching platform with those who so blatantly disregard God's clear command is confusing to those we lead. Some will call this "secondary separation" or "second-degree separation." I call it giving a clear sound in ministry and see it as having freedom in preaching by refusing to yoke up with people who have denied clear scriptural doctrines or have freely joined with those who do.

As I also noted in chapter 2, this practice is not unique to the ministry of Billy Graham. I noted there the more current example of Cary Nieuwhof inviting a Catholic priest to his church. I am now aware of Baptists inviting Nieuwhof to speak at their conferences. Think about it: first generation fundamentalists separated from Billy Graham because

---

11   Michael S. Hamilton, "How a Humble Evangelist Changed Christianity as We Know It," *Christianity Today,* April 2018, 26.

he allowed Catholics on his platform. Third and fourth generation fundamentalists are now inviting someone who shares his own pulpit with a Catholic to preach in their churches.

Additionally, there is a growing trend among Baptists to quote Catholic and other non-orthodox authors and to promote books, articles, and messages by those who share theological tents with liberals or Catholics. The spirit of desiring to bring the fundamentalists and modernists (or post-modernists) together for dialogue is still alive today—perhaps even more so than it was in the early days of New Evangelicalism. The openness to accepting liberal "interpretations" of fixed scriptural truths—such as creation and marriage—are ongoing. The slant toward a social gospel as the mission of the church continues. And discussions regarding the accuracy of biblical inspiration abound.

For example, in his book *Center Church,* author Timothy Keller emphasizes what he calls integrative ministry. While I don't oppose all of his concepts of incorporating service with the gospel, the roots of this integration are deeper. He is integrating the unbiblical concepts of the social gospel with the biblical principle of evangelism. Sometimes those exposed to this philosophy experience a diminishing emphasis of true soulwinning and evangelism in their church. Even more concerning to this discussion is the origin of the *Center Church* philosophy. Keller constantly quotes ecumenicist Lesslie Newbigin (a founder of the World Council of Churches) and other left-leaning theologians.

In describing his integration goals, Keller writes, "A gospel-centered church should combine the 'zeals' that are not typically seen together in the same church."[12] While he does not deny the need to lead others to Christ, his repeated emphasis to "disciple thousands of Christians to

---

12   Timothy Keller, *Center Church: Doing Balanced, Gospel-Centered Ministry in Your City* (Grand Rapids, MI: Zondervan, 2012), 292.

write plays, advance science, do creative journalism, begin effective and productive new businesses,"[13] etc. as specifically gospel ministry can blur the need to remember the basic and forgotten Great Commission of Matthew 28.

So the concerning connections forming are not simply ecclesiastical in nature. They are also philosophical. Overall, within those who identify as independent Baptists, there is a bridge forming between the Baptist position and the broader evangelical world with its many Bible versions, its overly-expansive emphasis on social issues, and its weak and permissive interpretations on the doctrine of God's grace. While not referred to anymore by the "New Evangelical" label, it is the classic New Evangelicalism of the 1960s.

What is really at stake here is the idea of reducing the truth—stripping it down to such a basic form that it would be hard to take a stand for or separate from anything. If the *only* things we believe and can stand for are the core truths of the gospel itself—the death, burial, and resurrection of Christ—and if other doctrines such as the inspiration and preservation of Scripture, the biblical makeup of the church, the Baptist distinctives, eternal security, personal holiness, biblically-centered worship, and more are non-essential and thus don't matter, then anyone who separates over these is labeled nitpicky and small-minded.

I don't doubt the sincerity of leaders who simply want to reach more people with the gospel and who see separation as an obstacle to doing so. What I do doubt, however, is their understanding of biblical separation and perception of the issues in a historical context. And I'm concerned over the direction these misunderstandings could take them.

Not only do I believe that the decisions to share a platform with those who deny (or who strongly identify themselves with those who deny) the

---

13   Ibid.

doctrines of God's Word violate scriptural principle, but I don't believe they have been pragmatically helpful over the long range. I know that the separatist position is not viewed favorably among the wider circle of Christendom. But inasmuch as it has been a biblical and a humble, obedient response to God's commands to contend for the faith (rather than preference or personality driven), it has not lacked for opportunities to preach the gospel, disciple converts, or fulfill the Great Commission.

On the contrary, I would contend that ecclesiastical separation combined with biblical unity in shared doctrine has historically promoted the spread of the gospel. In fact, two of the greatest strengths of the independent Baptist movement have been personal soulwinning and a fervency for missions. Indeed, God has given great fruit through these efforts.

THE WAY FORWARD

Those of us who share the passion to spread the gospel do well to learn from history as we have done in these past three chapters. For it is in understanding and appreciating the sacrifices of our spiritual fathers that we can make wise decisions and take sure steps on the path forward.

Here in the high desert of Southern California where I pastor, there are many dirt paths winding around Joshua trees, cacti, and sage brush. Some of these paths lead to an actual destination—a desert spring or watering hole, a road, or the top of a mountain. Some, however, simply meander throughout the desert leading to nowhere in particular—except further and further from where you started. When hiking in the desert, then, you need to be sure you are on a good path to have a confirmed direction.

This is the illustration God gave through the prophet Jeremiah to backsliding Israel: "Thus saith the LORD, Stand ye in the ways, and see, and ask for the old paths, where is the good way, and walk therein, and ye shall find rest for your souls" (Jeremiah 6:16). I realize some men have used this passage to divide over preference issues, but take a moment to consider the concepts in context that help us today. In this passage, God calls His people to pause and consider their direction. He gives them three commands:

Stand—This command to *stand ye in the ways* is not the same as the New Testament instruction to contend for the faith or stand for what is right. It is a command to pause and consider where you are going. It is a call to contemplate the spirit of your heart and direction of your life. In other words, don't keep following a path just because it is a path; that path may be a rabbit trail. Stop to consider.

See—This is a call to perception. Look across the horizon to where you are headed. Are you on a path marked by biblical truth? Or are you on a broad path of ecumenicalism? Are you on a path that uses the doctrines of God's Word as its signposts? Or are you on a path that measures its progress by the acceptance of the world?

Like paths in the desert, not all paths that look similar lead to the same destination. And in our case, the destination is future generations. Look ahead to consider where the trends and alliances of today will impact the churches our children will attend tomorrow.

Ask—As Jeremiah perceived the direction Israel was heading, he told them to instead *ask for the old paths*. The phrase "old paths" has sometimes been used out of context to refer to relatively-recent history (i.e. the old paths of Billy Sunday or the ministry methods of John R. Rice). But that's not how it is used here. Rather, Jeremiah was pleading with Israel to return to the paths of allegiance to God and a complete rejection of idolatry. We could apply the admonition today to walk in the paths of commitment to Christ-focused worship, New Testament truth, and contending for the faith. These paths, when we walk in them, lead us in a good way where we find rest for our souls.

My greatest desire is not to follow men or movements; it's not to preserve history or project my preferences into the future. My great desire is to lift up Christ to a lost world. It is to preach the "gospel of Christ: for it is the power of God unto salvation to every one that believeth" (Romans 1:16). To that end, I want to keep the faith and encourage others to do the same.

PART TWO

DISCERNING MINISTRY TRENDS

UNDERSTANDING TRENDS

L OOKING BACK AT PAST BATTLES for the truth gives perspective to the importance of holding to the truth, and it gives courage as we see others who have stood against doctrinal or practical compromise. But yesterday's issues aren't just history; they influence today's trends as well.

Ministry trends can be challenging to write about because they change so quickly—both in focus and in the terms used to discuss them. By the time this book is in your hands, the "hot" topics may already have shifted. But the biblical principles of gospel ministry remain the same. As we look at specific ministry trends in the next several chapters, I hope to point you to the unchanging biblical principles through which we should filter any trends.

Part of the reason that ministry trends shift is because our culture shifts as well. The culture in which we are attempting to reach people for Christ today is unraveling before our eyes. Notice just a few of its many challenges:

Biblical Illiteracy—It is not uncommon today to meet an adult who has little to no knowledge of basic biblical truths—including even an awareness of the biblical account of Adam and Eve, a working definition of sin, or a knowledge of the life of Christ. Even professing Christians know very little about what they believe or the Bible itself. A recent study by Gallup Poll presented staggering statistics:

- 22 percent of Americans believe the Bible is the actual Word of God and should be taken literally.
- 28 percent believe it is the actual Word of God, but with multiple possible interpretations.
- 28 percent believe the Bible is the inspired Word of God, but should not be taken literally.
- 18 percent believe it is an ancient book of legends, history, and moral precepts written by man.[1]

Breakdown of the Family—In 1960, 72 percent of all adults ages eighteen and older were married. Today that number is just 52 percent. Among all American adults, however, almost six in ten (57 percent) either currently live with their boyfriend/girlfriend or have previously done so. And 65 percent think it's a good idea.[2]

Rise in Pagan Practices—Like the cities of first-century Asia Minor described in 1 Peter 4:3, America today is turning to pagan practices. There is the worship of false gods (including a growing segment who actually identify as pagan or New Age), open sexuality, and the legalization of drugs.

---

1   Lydia Saad, "Three in Four in U.S. Still See the Bible as Word of God," *Gallup*, June 4, 2014, https://news.gallup.com/poll/170834/three-four-bible-word-god.aspx.
2   "Majority of Americans Now Believe in Cohabitation," *Barna Group*, June 24, 2016, https://www.barna.com/research/majority-of-americans-now-believe-in-cohabitation.

Hostility to Authority—Second Timothy 3 gives this indicator of the last days: "For men shall be lovers of their own selves, covetous, boasters, proud, blasphemers, disobedient to parents, unthankful, unholy" (2 Timothy 3:2). We are seeing an unprecedented and polarizing rise of hostility toward elected officials across our nation. Additionally, we're seeing growing hostility toward religious, and particularly Christian, leaders.

Apathy—There is a growing spiritual apathy around us. Nearly half of millennials (48 percent) qualify as post-Christian.[3] Nearly two-fifths of the nation's adult population (38 percent) now qualify as post-Christian (measured by people's identity, beliefs, and behaviors).[4]

Laodicean Churches—At the same time that hostility toward Christians is rising and culture is unraveling, Christians themselves seem to be unconcerned—or at least unconcerned with what really matters. Too many churches today are like the Laodicean church Jesus rebuked in Revelation 3:15–17: "I know thy works, that thou art neither cold nor hot: I would thou wert cold or hot. So then because thou art lukewarm, and neither cold nor hot, I will spue thee out of my mouth. Because thou sayest, I am rich, and increased with goods, and have need of nothing; and knowest not that thou art wretched, and miserable, and poor, and blind, and naked."

The city name *Laodicea* means "people's rights" or "justice for the people." And indeed, the decline in Christianity in America reveals many churches that are often concerned with their preferences and rights, but unconcerned with exalting Christ or reaching their communities with the gospel.

---

3   "The State of the Church 2016," *Barna Group*, September 15, 2016, https://www.barna.com/research/state-church-2016.

4   "Five Trends Among the Unchurched," *Barna Group*, October 9, 2014, https://www.barna.com/research/five-trends-among-the-unchurched.

An Associated Press article reported, "Nobody would have guessed the pace of change. . . . The Protestant majority that dominated American culture through U.S. history has dipped below 50 percent. . . . Liberal-leaning Protestant groups started shrinking earlier, but some evangelical churches are now in decline."[5]

According to statistics released in advance of the 2017 Southern Baptist Convention annual meeting, membership within SBC churches declined for the tenth straight year, while baptisms dropped to the lowest level in seventy years. Today there are one million fewer Southern Baptists than a decade ago.[6] I'd like to think that the statistics fare better for unaffiliated Baptists, but without any kind of centralized reporting, it's impossible to know. And I'm not sure that the independent churches as a whole are actually growing either.

As sad as these statistics are, what concerns me even more is that there seems to be indifference among spiritual leaders toward reaching unsaved people for Christ and contending for the faith. It seems that rather than lifting up the truth, self-preservation and self-promotion have become the themes among spiritual leaders. Pastors and leaders are often either overwhelmed by the needs of this unraveling culture or are caught up in it. Others are distracted by pettiness. Like Diotrephes who John said, "loveth to have the preeminence among them" (3 John 9), they desire control and so create and defend straw men issues which only serve to distract from the real concerns.

Where does this leave spiritual leaders who care for truth and desire to reach an unraveling culture with the gospel? Well, for starters, it should

5   Associated Press, "Evangelicals Feel Alienated, Anxious amid Declining Clout," *Fox News*, June 9, 2016, https://www.foxnews.com/us/evangelicals-feel-alienated-anxious-amid-declining-clout.

6   Bob Allen, "Southern Baptists Have Lost a Million Members in 10 Years," *Baptist News Global*, June 9, 2017, https://baptistnews.com/article/southern-baptists-lost-million-members-10-years/#.XaENxS2ZNBw.

leave us cautious. *Every* way is not the *right* way, and *every* trend does not lead to greater truth. It is a naive leader who believes that just because a leader, group, or style of ministry appears to be reaching people, the underlying philosophies and methods are biblical and will prove to be helpful over the long range. This is why we must evaluate ministry philosophies through a biblical paradigm.

PREFERENCES AND PRINCIPLES

As we work through these next few chapters, I want to assure you that these are not primarily about my ministry preferences. I have ministry preferences, as everyone does. But I want to focus here on biblical principles.

I believe in the autonomy of the local church and the responsibility of a pastor to lead it. In every church, there are times when change is necessary. Sometimes change is simply an expression of growth in grace. Sometimes it is a new idea that is biblical and helpful. But some of the current trends of change have become alarming to me. Specifically, the spirit behind some of the change has been alarming.

It's not *just* dropping service times, abandoning organized soulwinning, or using the terminology of neo-orthodox teachers. It's the combined effect of these decisions and more that is contributing to a blurred identity in many of today's leaders. While they talk about the fact that preferences don't matter (and in many cases they don't), there is a spirit of anger and a rallying of people who are against those who don't share *their* preferences. And what concerns me most is that in this tension—this pushing against perceived impositions—battles that have already been fought and philosophies that have already been weighed and found wanting are resurfacing with new labels and terms and being eagerly received by a new generation.

This is why when we consider ministry trends, we must filter them through biblical principles, and we must each develop a ministry philosophy that is firmly anchored in truth—not developed through trends. As in all areas of ministry philosophy, the goal is biblical discernment (Philippians 1:9–10).

DOCTRINE AND DIRECTION

Ministry trends have greater significance than the surface methods or even the philosophies behind those ministry methods. The doctrine that drives them is important.

Historically, being independent Baptist was about believing Baptist doctrine and being willing to separate from those who preached or taught unbiblical doctrine or practice. But what has happened among too many unaffiliated Baptists today is a claim that the *only* doctrines that are significant are those related to salvation itself.

This is where church planting and collaborative movements with broad doctrinal affiliations, including Baptists, Presbyterians, Pentecostal, non-denominational, and other groups, concern me. Through their conferences, websites, and networks, there is a wide gamut of doctrinal representations—with everyone willing to set their distinctions aside.

I'm for the gospel, and I'm for the spread of the gospel. But I am an independent Baptist for more reasons than believing in salvation by grace through faith alone. I am a Baptist because I embrace *all* of the Baptist distinctives. We could list these in a more thorough way, but below is the basic acrostic that is commonly used. I like it for its simplicity, and I think it covers our purposes here:

- *Biblical Authority in all matters of faith and practice* (2 Timothy 3:16; John 17:17; Acts 17:11; Hebrews 4:12; 2 Peter 1:20–21)
- *Autonomy or self-governing power of the local church* (Colossians 1:18; Acts 13–14, 20:19–30; Ephesians 1:22–23; Revelation 1:11–20)
- *Priesthood of believers* (Hebrews 4:14–16; 1 Timothy 2:5–6; 1 Peter 1:16; 2:5–10)
- *Two offices within the church* (Philippians 1:1; Acts 6:1–7; 20:17, 28–30; 1 Timothy 3:1–13; Titus 1:6–9; 1 Peter 5:1–4)
- *Individual soul liberty* (Romans 10:9–17, 14:1–23)
- *Saved and baptized church membership* (Acts 2:41–47; 1 Corinthians 12:12)
- *Two ordinances—baptism and the Lord's Table* (Matthew 28:19; 1 Corinthians 11:23–26; Acts 2:38–43, 8:36–38; Romans 6:1–6)
- *Separation of church and state* (Matthew 22:21; Acts 5:29–31; Romans 13:1–4)

As we look at various ministry trends, it is relative to our discussion to notice the doctrinal issues that drive these trends and the doctrinal beliefs of their key leaders. Doctrine or practice that is significantly different from basic Baptist beliefs should, at the least, be taken into account when evaluating the direction of that trend.

Most ministry trends don't only lead to a single ministry idea or helpful method, but they also lead in a direction. Often in these days we see ministry ideas form a new contextualization, which forms a new ecclesiastical cooperation that leads to new biblical interpretations. I'm all for borrowing good ideas, but I caution you to be discerning of underlying doctrine and direction.

MOTIVES AND METHODS

When it comes to ministry, both motives *and* methods matter. I've heard well-meaning leaders argue one against the other.

Some say that *how* you do ministry doesn't matter as long as your motives are pure. For instance, let's say you give the gospel via a worldly method, but your heart is pure in wanting people to be saved. At least the people who got saved are now believers.

Others say that *why* you do what you do doesn't matter as long as there is fruit as a result. For instance, if you share the gospel with someone who trusts Christ but your motive in doing so was prideful, at least the person is still saved. In both cases, the result is fruit—so what's the big deal, right?

The reality is that God holds us responsible for both our motives and our methods. Consider King Jehoshaphat, one of the "good kings" of Judah. The biblical commentary, both at the beginning and end of his reign, is that he walked in the ways of the Lord and departed not from them. Furthermore, the Bible tells us that he did this from his heart: "And his heart was lifted up in the ways of the Lord" (2 Chronicles 17:6). God greatly blessed Jehoshaphat and the nation of Judah for this heart-driven pursuit of the Lord.

Yet, pure-hearted as Jehoshaphat was, he lacked discernment and joined in affinity with the kings of Israel—first Ahab and then Ahaziah. In both of those instances, God sent a prophet to confront him for his actions (2 Chronicles 19:2–3, 20:37). As the prophet Jehu corrected Jehoshaphat's methods, he even referenced Jehoshaphat's good motives. In the same breath as proclaiming "wrath [is] upon thee from before the Lord," the prophet said "thou . . . hast prepared thine heart to seek God."

> And Jehu the son of Hanani the seer went out to meet him, and said
> to king Jehoshaphat, Shouldest thou help the ungodly, and love them

that hate the LORD? *therefore is wrath upon thee from before the LORD.* Nevertheless there are good things found in thee, in that thou hast taken away the groves out of the land, *and hast prepared thine heart to seek God.*

—2 CHRONICLES 19:2–3

Jehoshaphat could have argued, as so many do today, "But my *heart* is right with God." And he would have been right. But his motives *and* his methods mattered to God. Jehoshaphat's philosophy of "peace with Israel at all costs" ran contrary to God's revealed Word. It also brought terrible repercussions in his own life and, more tragically, in the life of his son who married Ahab's daughter and turned away from the Lord (2 Chronicles 21:4–6).

The lesson for us? Although our hearts and our motives are crucial aspects to the direction of our ministries, even with pure motives, our ministry philosophies and methods can be wrong. We cannot pragmatically argue that the ends justify the means; and we should not pragmatically follow every ministry trend that appears to be reaching people with the gospel.

Paul wrote to the church at Philippi that he prayed they would be "sincere *and* without offence till the day of Christ" (Philippians 1:10). He wanted them to have the pure motive of love for Christ as they served Him as well as great discernment in how they did it (verse 9).

Labels and terms used to discuss ministry trends often have a wide range in meaning or perception. Because of the spectrum of use, it's usually impossible to either commend or condemn a simple term. In the chapters ahead, however, my goal is to drill deeper than a surface verbiage and examine the doctrinal and practical implications of ministry around current trends.

CHAPTER SEVEN

CONTEXTUALIZATION TRENDS

O N April 4, 1819, after nearly seven years in Burma (including three years of intense language study and a year translating the gospel of Matthew), Adoniram and Ann Judson held their first public worship service in the Burmese language. Fifteen men attended.

Less than three months later, Judson baptized his first convert, Moung Nau. Over the next year, he would see nine more people trust Christ as Savior and follow the Lord in believer's baptism.

Judson, who worked hard to adapt to the Burmese culture, built a *zayat*—a bamboo and thatch structure, patterned after the traditional Burmese zayats from which Buddhist priests would teach and where Buddhist followers would worship—near his home. It was a place where a passerby could stop for conversation and to ask questions, and it became the place where the Judsons held public worship services.

But Judson, as anxious as he was to adapt and show deference to his adopted culture, was also careful that he not compromise his message. He took care to distinguish his zayat from that of the Buddhist priests. In his diary, after he recorded the building and purposes of the zayat, he noted that it "is whitewashed, to distinguish it from the other zayats around us."[1]

Judson's adaptation to culture without compromising his message is a reminder that contextualization, as we call it today, is not new, and it need not be ungodly. We need to reach people around us with the gospel, and we must connect truth to their hearts in a way that is relevant and understandable in their current context.

In fact, all of us use contextualization to some extent, even if we don't use that term. For example, if you employ different teaching methods for a Vacation Bible School than you do for Sunday morning church service, you contextualize. The apostle Paul used different procedures in sharing the gospel based on if his primary audience in a particular location was Jewish or Gentile. Yet no matter what methods he employed, Paul never changed his message—it was always salvation by grace through faith in Christ. He contextualized his presentation to convey truth to his audience. But he didn't contextualize the message itself.

So, in what ways can *we* adapt to culture? In what ways is adapting helpful, and in what ways does it run counter to our message?

DEFINING CONTEXTUALIZATION

Contextualization speaks of what we will affirm or not affirm from culture in our presentation of truth. Sometimes it involves addition as

---

1   Jason G. Duesing, *Adoniram Judson: A Bicentennial Appreciation of the Pioneer American Missionary* (Nashville, TN: B&H Books, 2012), 139.

we personally take on an aspect of our surroundings (such as Adoniram Judson or Hudson Taylor did on the mission field), and sometimes it involves subtraction as we set aside a right or privilege in order to better communicate truth (such as Paul did by saying he would not eat meat offered to idols in order to not offend another believer, 1 Corinthians 8:13).

When we seek to minister in a relevant context, our goal is to be like the scuba diver who is submerged in water but breathes air. He adapts to his environment, but at the same time he takes the lifeline of his own environment with him. Our "environment" or "air" is the very Word of God. So yes, we need to understand the people around us and relate God's Word to their hearts. But we need to do so in the context of a biblical ministry philosophy.

For our purposes in this chapter, let's define a few terms.

Content
Scripture passage,
truth, or principle

Under Contextualization
Teaching truth without
understanding the audience

Over Contextualization
Teaching one truth in violation
of another truth

Contextualization
Connecting the truth to hearts in
an understandable way

Content is a specific Bible passage, truth, or principle we are attempting to teach. It may be the gospel, or it may be a sermon series on marriage or a verse-by-verse study of an epistle. Regardless, it is the message we are trying to convey, not the medium by which we do it.

Contextualization is our attempt to connect this truth with a heart. It may be an illustration about a firefighter giving his life to save another, or it may be themed décor on the platform or an interactive website for the church family to engage in throughout the week.

Under contextualization is attempting to teach truth, but not understanding the audience to whom you're presenting it. This would be the junior church teacher who teaches a lengthy Bible study on the book of Galatians. It could be a soulwinner who assumes the person to whom he is witnessing understands the meaning of sin and has basic Bible knowledge.

Over contextualization is attempting to connect truth with a heart but in a method that violates another truth. This could be where a church uses hard rock music to draw people to a gospel service. Or it could be a pastor giving illustrations from R-rated movies in his attempts to be contextually understood.

My favorite way to think of these terms is the illustration of a gift and its wrapping.

The *content* is the gift itself—the truth of God's Word.

Contextualization is the packaging—how we present the truth.

Under contextualization is barely packaging the gift at all, making it uninviting so no one is curious to see what is inside.

Over contextualization is packaging that distracts from or excludes the gift—methods that contradict the truth or presentations that are without substance.

The danger in either over contextualization or under contextualization is that we get so focused on the packaging (or on our pride in not packaging) that we forget the gift. Indeed, many churches with cool technology, awesome concerts, and great coffee are seeing fewer conversions. On the other hand, there are churches that take pride in their standards and fundamental doctrine that are also seeing fewer people trust Christ and become mature Christians. We must never forget that contextualization is only a tool and never a target. The power is in the gospel and in the moving of the Holy Spirit (Romans 1:16; Acts 1:8).

Like so many areas of ministry philosophy, there is a ditch on both sides of the contextualization road. And as is so often the case, it seems that most leaders consider themselves to be balanced and anyone to their right or left to be in the ditch. Consequently, there are a lot of accusations hurled from both ditches.

We should be honest enough to admit that where there is not a clear violation of Scripture, it can be hard to define what is helpful and what is compromise. Somewhere between what is clearly under contextualization and what is clearly over contextualization lie many preference issues. So we should be careful to give grace to one another and to recognize that not everyone who does things differently than we do is on a "slippery slope." They may just have a difference of interpretation, opinion, or preference on a particular issue.

OVER CONTEXTUALIZATION

The tendency to move toward over contextualization is not so much in the *premise* of contextualizing truth, but in the *application* of where, when, and how we do it. When are we providing helpful context for truth, and when are we compromising the very truth we're trying to teach?

To be sure, the expressions of over contextualization change as culture changes. But I suggest three common indicators:

Affirming ungodly aspects of a culture

Remember that contextualization speaks of what we will affirm or not affirm from culture. Obviously, not every aspect of any culture is sinful. But affirming ungodly aspects of culture can lead to syncretism where we begin to limit our doctrine in order to blend in.

The definition of *syncretism* is "the amalgamation or attempted amalgamation of different religions, cultures, or schools of thought."[2] Syncretism begins to take place when we seek to blend the truth with culture—perhaps even with the motive of making truth more palatable. But when we are not willing to allow the truth to confront beliefs and practices that are clearly against Scripture, we're no longer leading people biblically.

This syncretism seems to be what took place in Israel after Assyria took them captive. "They feared the LORD, and served their own gods, after the manner of the nations whom they carried away from thence" (2 Kings 17:33). Eventually, the Israelites who remained in Palestine not only married unbelievers (their descendents became the Samaritans), but developed a confusing, blended worship with them. When Jesus discussed worship with the Samaritan woman at the well, He pointedly said, "Ye worship ye know not what" (John 4:22).

Doctrinal syncretism takes place today as well. One author warned that the term *contextualization* can be used to validate doctrinal error. He wrote, "Some, for example, have advocated that contextualization in the Islamic context means downplaying the deity of Christ or, among postmoderns, downplaying the doctrine of sin or the call to repentance."[3]

But doctrinal syncretism shows up in more than outright heresy. There is also the overt compromise of refusing to take a clear stand on issues that are abundantly clear in Scripture, such as homosexuality. Over the past decade and longer, as our culture has openly embraced same-

---

2   *Lexico*, s.v. "syncretism," accessed October 11, 2019, https://www.lexico.com/en/definition/syncretism.
3   Timothy Tennent, *Invitation to World Missions* (Grand Rapids: Kregel Academic Publications, 2010), 351.

sex relationships, churches have been growing increasingly silent on this issue as they try to blend into the culture.

Sometime back, Brian Houston, the lead pastor of Hillsong Church, a Pentecostal church in Sydney with campuses around the world, was asked in an interview what the Bible says about homosexuality. He answered ambiguously: "The real issues in people's lives are too important for us to just reduce it down to a 'yes' or 'no' answer in a media outlet."[4]

More recently, Christian singer Lauren Daigle was asked in an interview what she believes about homosexuality and responded, "I can't say one way or the other, I'm not God."[5] I'm not God either, but I can pretty easily say what He clearly said in Romans 1.

These kinds of conversations remind me of what Howard Hendricks said almost four decades ago, "In the midst of a generation screaming for answers, Christians are stuttering."[6] This loss of clarity, however, is not just in regards to homosexuality; it is also related to abortion, drunkenness, and other moral issues that are clear in Scripture.

A few years ago, Carl Lentz, a Hillsong pastor in New York City, made news with the headline, "Concerns Raised as Photos Resurface of Hillsong's Hipster 'Pastor' Carl Lentz Slamming Shots with Justin Bieber."[7] A few weeks later, Lentz was interviewed regarding the issue of abortion and gave an unclear answer. The next day's headline describing

---

4   Jonathan Merritt, "Hillsong's Brian Houston Says Church Won't Take Public Position on LGBT Issues," *Religion News Service*, October 16, 2014, https://religionnews.com/2014/10/16/hillsongs-brian-houston-says-church-lgbtissues.

5   https://www1.cbn.com/cbnnews/2018/december/christian-singer-lauren-daigle-on-homosexuality-i-cant-say-one-way-or-the-other-im-not-god

6   Howard Hendricks, *Taking a Stand: What God Can Do through Ordinary You!* (Multnoma Press: Colorado Springs, 1983), 12.

7   Heather Clark, "Concerns Raised as Photos Resurface of Hillsong's Hipster 'Pastor' Carl Lentz Slamming Shots With Justin Bieber," *Christian News Network*, July 31, 2017, https://christiannews.net/2017/07/31/concerns-raised-as-photos-resurface-of-hillsongs-hipster-pastor-carl-lentz-slamming-shots-with-justin-bieber.

the interview read, "Hillsong Pastor Carl Lentz Refuses to Say If Abortion is Sinful: 'Live to Your Own Convictions.'"[8]

Whether it be related to abortion, drunkenness, or homosexuality, how can a preacher of God's Word tell people to "live to their own convictions" on matters that are absolutely clear in Scripture? It doesn't matter how well-intentioned we may be; when we cannot give a clear answer related to biblical truth, we lose our authority to speak the truth.

Conversations around contextualization often include Paul's statement in 1 Corinthians 9:22, "To the weak became I as weak, that I might gain the weak: I am made all things to all men, that I might by all means save some." For anyone who loves the gospel and wants to reach lost people for Christ, that last phrase "that I might by all means save some" deeply resounds in their hearts. As a stand-alone statement, the verse could imply that Paul was willing to be and do anything culturally relevant to reach people with the gospel.

Indeed, Paul was willing to go through great hardship to see people saved. The context of this verse, however, reveals that Paul did not put himself in a position where the method by which he communicated the truth contradicted the truth. In fact, it shows that he actually set aside his personal liberties to be able to reach more people. "For though I be free from all men, yet have I made myself servant unto all, that I might gain the more" (verse 19). In the verses following, Paul describes how he was willing to follow the law of Moses while with the Jews, even though he knew he was free from it. And when with Gentiles, he was willing to set aside his familiar practices related to the Jewish law. In other words, Paul

---

8   Micaiah Bilger, "Hillsong Pastor Carl Lentz Refuses to Say If Abortion is Sinful: 'Live to Your Own Convictions,'" *LifeNews.com*, November 6, 2017, https://www.lifenews. com/2017/11/06/hillsong-pastor-carl-lentz-refuses-to-say-if-abortion-is-sinful-live-to-your-own-convictions.

was not using worldly methods to please and attract men; rather he was limiting his liberty so as to not distract men from his message.

God has called us to be salt and light in the midst of a crooked and perverse nation (Matthew 5:13–16, Philippians 2:15). We must love the people we are trying to reach. We must be willing to leave our comfort zones and connect with lost people. We should show Christlike grace and give generous hospitality to our neighbors. But we must not kid ourselves that by engaging in the sinful aspects of culture we'll have better opportunity to free those who are already taken captive by Satan.

Two centuries ago, Charles Spurgeon said it well: "There are some, in these apostate days, who think that the church cannot do better than to come down to the world to learn her ways, follow her maxims, and acquire her 'culture.' In fact, the notion is that the world is to be conquered by our conformity to it. This is as contrary to Scripture as the light is to the darkness."[9]

Man pleasing

Much of over contextualization has at its foundation the sin of man pleasing. That's not to say that man pleasing doesn't express itself in other ways, too. (We'll see another side of man pleasing as we look at under contextualization.) But pertinent to this discussion, if we make man the target in ministry, we will often compromise truth.

Those who have become frustrated with practices of separation accuse separatists of worrying too much about what men think. They believe that sometimes a separatist adapts certain standards or convictions simply to please his mentors rather than because of what the Bible really teaches. Sometimes these accusations are true. But I think it is also fair to point

9   Charles Haddon Spurgeon, *The Metropolitan Tabernacle Pulpit: Sermons, Parts 369-380* (London: Passmore & Alabaster, 1886), 148.

out the phenomenon that Baptists fleeing "man pleasing" environments are often seeking to please yet a different group of men with their new-found forms of contextualization.

I remember when Chief Justice Antonin Scalia, speaking to a 1996 audience, said, "Devout Christians are destined to be regarded as fools in modern society."[10] It made news at the time, and the secular media mocked it.[11] But his words were prophetic. So often, churches today are trying to blend in with the world, and their premise of doing it to "reach the world" is not always clarity in message, but is to avoid the stigma of being an out-of-step Christian on "the wrong side of history."

David Wells wrote, "A soft, shapeless Christianity ready to adapt to any worldview may enjoy initial success, but it will soon be overtaken and lose its interest [when] . . . those outside the faith soon see that they can reap Christian benefits on purely secular grounds without paying whatever small price is being asked for the adapted version of this faith."[12]

This is nothing more than what was called the seeker-sensitive movement of the 1990s . . . and it reaches back even further to the New Evangelical movement of the 1950s. The basic idea is to give people what they want in order to get them to want what you have. But if the price of giving them what they want includes giving up biblical holiness, it becomes a man-pleasing method that doesn't bear long-term fruit.

This plays out in a variety of ways, one of which is an unwillingness to preach against the specifics of sin, while accommodating the church to

---

10 Everett Piper, "Scalia an Obedient, Humble Follower of Christ," *Bartlesville Examiner-Enterprise*, February 16, 2016, https://www.examiner-enterprise.com/article/20160216/opinion/302169972.

11 Colman McCarthy, "Martyrs in Their Own Minds," *The Washington Post*, April 23, 1996, https://www.washingtonpost.com/archive/lifestyle/1996/04/23/martyrs-in-their-own-minds/8884f015-2004-4243-8b03-d91a895ff719.

12 David F. Wells, *The Courage to Be Protestant* (Grand Rapids, MI: Wm. B. Eerdmans Publishing Company, 2008), 94.

society rather than to the Word of God. Ernest Pickering notes that in the paragraph below, including a quote from David Wells:

> New Evangelicals have specialized in "side-stepping controversy." What we need, according to many of these leaders, is not *confrontation*, but *contextualization*. "What is required is not merely a practical application of biblical doctrine but a translation of that doctrine into a conceptuality that meshes with the reality of our social structures and the patterns of life dominant in contemporary life." He seems to be saying that the church should adapt, that it should accommodate. The church should present its message within the acceptable patterns of contemporary society.[13]

If we refuse to preach against the sins of the day, we become tacit accomplices to it. R. Kent Hughes wrote, "[The modern church] is lacking in its ability to remain uncontaminated by the unchristian thinking and morality of contemporary culture."[14] I'm afraid he is right.

Whether it be in doctrine or practice, contextualizing truth should never be done in a way to remove the distinction between the church and the world.

Devaluing preaching

In our post-Christian society, there is a cultural distaste for preaching. And in an effort to gain seekers, many preachers are de-emphasizing preaching—the declaring of God's Word that leads people to a decision.

---

13 Ernest Pickering, *The Tragedy of Compromise: The Origin and Impact of the New Evangelicalism* (Greenville, SC: Bob Jones University Press, 1994), 25.. Quoted material is from David Wells, "An American Evangelical Theology: The Painful Transition from Theoria to Praxis," in *Evangelicalism and Modern America*, ed. George Marsden (Grand Rapids, MI: Wm. B. Eerdmans Publishing Company, 1984), 90.

14 R. Kent Hughes, *Set Apart: Calling a Worldly Church to a Godly Life* (Wheaton, IL: Crossway Books, 2003), 10.

When you add to these dynamics some of the either biblically-shallow or overly-authoritarian preaching that some have experienced in "fundamental" churches, some younger preachers themselves also seem to have a distaste for preaching.

Jeff Amsbaugh pointed out these concerns in an article voicing his observations about gospel-centered interpretations of ministry, specifically in The Gospel Coalition (TGC) circles:

> To be sure, the scholarly approach, the cultural relevance, and the calm spirit pervading the TGC movement has much to commend, and it is understandable why some young fundamentalists who are disenfranchised with mean-spirited and intellectually-inferior preaching are drawn to it. I wonder, however, if the pendulum has swung too much in the opposite direction.[15]

I pointed to this tendency twenty years ago in *Guided by Grace:* "While shameful pulpits where people are named and ridiculed do exist, another tragedy is developing. Specifically, cynically minded parishioners view all preaching as bashing, all strong leadership as authoritarian."[16]

One pastor recently devalued over half of the Bible itself in an effort to connect with unchurched hearers. In a Sunday morning message, Pastor Andy Stanley said, "Peter, James, Paul elected to unhitch the Christian faith from their Jewish scriptures, and my friends, we must as well."[17] The reality is that as many as eight hundred verses in the New Testament are references from the Old Testament. In an article about Stanley's statement,

---

15 Jeff Amsbaugh, "Observations about the Gospel-Centered Interpretation of Ministry," *Ministry* 127, May 21, 2018, http://ministry127.com/pastoral-leadership/observations-about-the-gospel-centered-interpretation-of-ministry.

16 Paul Chappell, *Guided by Grace* (Murfreesboro, TN: Sword of the Lord Publishers, 2000), 58.

17 Andy Stanley, "Aftermath, Part 3: Not Difficult," video, 39:44, posted by "Andy Stanley," April 30, 2018, https://youtu.be/pShxFTNRCWI.

The Christian Post pointed out, "In his zeal to reach the unchurched and to recover those burned by traditional religion, Pastor Stanley forgets that the Old Testament also tells us the story of Israel, including Israel's blessed future. (For the record, the story of Israel was important for the Gentile converts as well; that's why Paul could freely reference the Passover in his writings; see 1 Corinthians 5:7–8.)"[18]

Andy Stanley's motive may have been noble—to help unsaved people develop interest in the gospel. But in his eagerness for relevance, he missed truth. (Even Albert Mohler, who is a leader of Stanley's own Southern Baptist Convention, argues that Stanley is walking a road that those moving toward heresy walk.)[19]

Another way in which preaching can be devalued is in a heavy reliance on apologetics to bring unbelievers to faith. To be sure, our belief in Christ is a reasonable faith. God does not bypass our minds when He instructs us to believe in Him but invites, "Come now, and let us reason together" (Isaiah 1:18). I appreciate people such as Lee Strobel who wrote *The Case for Christ* and others who have carefully studied and articulated the historic, scientific, and logical arguments for the Christian faith rooted in what we might call "general revelation" (Romans 1:20). But the use of apologetics should never replace the actual sharing of the gospel itself—the death, burial, and resurrection of Christ for our sins (1 Corinthians 15:3–4). And an understanding of logic or apologetics should never cause us to pull away from or look down on the bold declaration of the gospel (1 Corinthians 1:21).

---

18   Michael Brown, "No, Pastor Andy Stanley, We Should Not Unhitch Ourselves from the Old Testament," *Christian Post*, May 11, 2018, https://www.christianpost.com/voice/no-pastor-andy-stanley-we-should-not-unhitch-ourselves-from-the-old-testament.html.

19   Albert Mohler, "Getting 'Unhitched' from the Old Testament? Andy Stanley Aims at Heresy," *Albert Mohler*, August 10, 2018, https://albertmohler.com/2018/08/10/getting-unhitched-old-testament-andy-stanley-aims-heresy.

Regardless of the form—affirming too much of culture, man pleasing, or a de-emphasis on preaching—over contextualization does not help the truth, but hinders it.

UNDER CONTEXTUALIZATION

If over contextualization elevates the world over truth, under contextualization elevates tradition over truth. Over contextualization diminishes doctrine, but under contextualization elevates tradition to the place of doctrine.

I think it would be fair to say that some of the over contextualization taking place among independent Baptists may be an overcorrection to under contextualization that has sometimes been held up as biblical standard. When I was growing up, independent Baptists were innovators. They were determined to reach people with the gospel and were creative in using multi-faceted approaches, perhaps the hallmark of which was the bus ministry. Back then, evangelistically-minded leaders of other denominations borrowed ideas from us for reaching their communities. Today, it seems to be the other way around, and I believe that is because we are sometimes unwilling to contextualize past the 1960s.

Emphasizing a style from sixty years ago to prove to other people that you have not changed does not always further the gospel. Being unaware of the needs or unwilling to consider the people where you serve is not a virtue. For instance, I pastor in Southern California. When I preach on marriage and parenting, if I'm not aware of the reality that many first-generation Christians in our church have been divorced and remarried and are parenting blended families, I'll preach messages that sound unconnected to their daily lives. That's not to say that what the Bible teaches concerning the home is different today than it was forty years ago.

The Bible hasn't changed, and its truth is *particularly* relevant for families in a culture that consistently undermines the home. However, when I understand my community and the unique needs of today's culture, I'll preach with challenges a single parent faces in mind. I'll be more sensitive to considering the needs of a blended family when it comes to preaching about favoritism and unconditional love.

If we don't understand the culture in which we serve, we tend to preach and minister to please our mentors or our peers rather than to please the Lord. In many ways, under contextualization can have man pleasing at its root just as over contextualization does. The difference is that it is simply a different set of men.

THE BIBLICAL BALANCE

So how can we contextualize the gospel message without compromising biblical truth or obscuring it through tradition? How can we engage our world without relinquishing our convictions?

I suggest four balancing truths:

The church is a called out assembly.

When a church attempts to be like the world in order to reach the world, it loses its distinctiveness and its ability to lead people away from the world to Christ. It is not the business of the church to adapt Christ to men, but men to Christ. This is why God gives implicit commands to Christians to keep themselves from getting tangled up in the world: "Pure religion and undefiled before God and the Father is this, To visit the fatherless and widows in their affliction, *and to keep himself unspotted from the world*" (James 1:27).

Many Baptists today are following the idea of designing a service to make unbelievers comfortable, rather than with the primary purposes of glorifying God and preaching the Word. In the book *Deep and Wide: Creating Churches Unchurched People Love to Attend* Andy Stanley suggests, "In the pre-service experience, comfortable takes precedence over theological." He gives an example a few paragraphs later: "We choose all of our pre-service music with a first-time, unchurched person in mind. We include a mixture of familiar secular and not-so-familiar worship tunes as people enter the worship center."[20] While making guests comfortable and welcome is important, allowing anything to take precedence over biblical truth leads to compromise.

We should remember that the men and women who have changed the world have been the men and women the world could not change. No matter how deeply we care for others, when we allow our lives to become a reflection of the world, we lose our ability to serve those in need the way God has called us to do it.

We are not called to reinvent the church; we are instructed to *be* the church. "Is the church ours to reinvent, or is it God's? Does the head of the church have anything to say, or do the consultants have the last word? Was the church first invented by a previous generation, so that it is our job to do it again, or is the church's real need for the revival and reformation that can only come from God?"[21]

To be sure, there is a fine line between *relevance* and *conformity*. We want to be relevant without conforming to the world. Romans 12:2 directly commands us, "And be not conformed to this world: but be ye transformed by the renewing of your mind, that ye may prove what is

---

20 Andy Stanley, *Deep and Wide: Creating Churches Unchurched People Love to Attend* (Grand Rapids, MI: Zondervan, 2012) chapter 10, kindle edition.

21 Os Guinness, *Prophetic Untimeliness: A Challenge to the Idol of Relevance* (Grand Rapids, MI: Baker Books, 2003), 65.

that good, and acceptable, and perfect, will of God." The word *conformed* in this verse is translated from the Greek word *syschematizo* which means "to fashion after the same pattern, to change from the outside." It speaks of being squeezed into a mold.

Relevance may be something that those who under contextualize need to give greater attention to, but it should never be the driving force of a church. Yet, in many ways, relevance has become the obsession of the modern church, and truth has been lost in its pursuit.

Relevance does not supersede holiness. And when relevance is used to justify sinful appetites and behaviors, it's wrong. For instance, watching a popular R-rated movie to reference it in preaching doesn't help me reach people for Christ; it weakens my sensitivity to the Holy Spirit. And, quite honestly, hearing illustrations from these movies doesn't help a new believer's growth in grace either.

This doesn't mean that every aspect of a culture is sinful. There are aspects of every culture that, in spite of the fall, are reflections of God's goodness, beauty, and creativity. Mountain climbing in Seattle is not a sin, nor is the symphony in New York. But we *must* cry aloud against the ungodly aspects of our culture. And we must recognize that much of the philosophy, music, habits, and practices of our day are not harmless "expressions of culture"; they are godless, sensual, and sinful, and they are to be avoided. First John 2:15 is clear about this: "Love not the world, neither the things that are in the world. If any man love the world, the love of the Father is not in him." That last phrase is especially sobering.

Jerry Bridges wrote, "The world . . . is characterized by the subtle and relentless pressure it brings to bear upon us to conform to its values and practices. It creeps up on us little by little. What was once unthinkable becomes thinkable, then doable, and finally acceptable to society at large.

Sin becomes respectable, and so Christians are no more than five to ten years behind the world in embracing most sinful practices."[22]

We must remember that true discipleship requires taking up Christ's cross: "Then said Jesus unto his disciples, If any man will come after me, let him deny himself, and take up his cross, and follow me" (Matthew 16:24).

To quote Os Guinness,

> The faith world of John Wesley, Jonathan Edwards, John Jay . . . is disappearing. In its place a new evangelicalism is arriving in which therapeutic self-concern overshadows knowing God, spirituality displaces theology, end-times escapism crowds out day-to-day discipleship, marketing triumphs over mission, references to opinion polls outweigh reliance on biblical exposition, concerns for power and relevance are more obvious than concern for piety and faithfulness, talk of reinventing the church has replaced prayer for revival, and the characteristic evangelical passion for missionary enterprise is overpowered by the all-consuming drive to sustain the multiple business empires of the booming evangelical subculture.[23]

In their book *UnChristian,* authors David Kinnaman and Gabe Lyons highlight a number of troubling statistics from an extensive study by the Barna Research Group of those born between 1965 and 2002. Included are two statistics that show how those outside the church view those within: Of the non-Christians surveyed, 84 percent said they personally know at least one committed Christian. Yet just 15 percent thought the lifestyles of those Christ-followers were significantly different from the norm.[24]

---

22 Jerry Bridges, *The Discipline of Grace* (Colorado Springs, CO: NavPress, 1994), 202–203.
23 Guinness, *Prophetic Untimeliness: A Challenge to the Idol of Relevance,* 54.
24 David Kinnaman and Gabe Lyons, *unChristian: What a New Generation Really Thinks about Christianity . . . and Why It Matters* (Grand Rapids, MI: Baker Books, 2012), 48.

This is not a book on specific standards of separation or the doctrine of sanctification. But we must recognize that our personal lifestyle choices either reflect our love for God or our love for the world. And the same is true of our basic ministry methods. While many people will draw a line in different places, our foundational conviction must be that we don't want to *blend in* but to *stand out.* We are "a chosen generation, a royal priesthood, an holy nation, a peculiar people" with the incredible privilege and responsibility to "shew forth the praises of him who hath called you out of darkness into his marvellous light" (1 Peter 2:9). We are "strangers and pilgrims" and, as such, must "abstain from fleshly lusts, which war against the soul" (1 Peter 2:11).

We don't want to join the world, but we want to offer hope to those in darkness that they can know the light of knowing Christ, walking with Him, and being transformed by Him. Author R. Kent Hughes said it this way: "We must lay this to heart: A worldly church cannot and will not reach the world. The church must be distinct from the world to reach the world. We must set ourselves apart to God if we hope to reach the world. In a word, the only hope for us and the lost world is a holy church."[25] Several paragraphs later, Hughes continued, "Setting ourselves apart from the world so that we might reach the world is not so much a series of noes as much as it is an immense yes to Christ and all that he gives."[26]

Our identity as the called out people of God must never be compromised in how we deliver our message. This is where Adoniram Judson—two hundred years ago and half a world away—got it right. He wanted to bring the gospel to a foreign people without causing them to dismiss it as a foreigner's faith. So he looked for common ground

---

25   R. Kent Hughes, *Set Apart: Calling a Worldly Church to a Godly Life* (Wheaton, IL: Crossway, 2003), 17.

26   Ibid., 22.

from which he could communicate—a zayat. But even on that common ground, he was careful to make it distinct—not foreign, but distinct.

This is where we must exercise caution as well. We want to reach people where they are without communicating that God is distant and Christianity relates to a bygone era. But we do want to communicate that God is holy, and He can save us from the bondage of a godless life to experience the freedom of life in Him.

Creativity is not compromise.

We must not demand uniformity in matters of contextualization. As we saw earlier, there is a realm of preference that is not directly addressed by Scripture. If every time a leader within our Baptist circles tries to think outside the box and use creativity in reaching a particular demographic, the rest of us cry out, "worldly!" we'll squelch the pioneering spirit which we need.

I love the story in Mark 2:3–5 of the four men who were so determined to bring their paralyzed friend to Jesus that they broke up a roof to do it. This is the kind of determination and out-of-the-box thinking we need today—not conformity, but creativity.

We must work to understand the communities in which we serve and bring creative avenues for ministry. This might include a single moms support group, a service schedule that meets commuters' needs, a neighborhood barbecue, or meals for the homeless. It might be a message series based on topics specifically relevant to people in your community, or it may be satellite campuses for outreach.

I remember twenty years ago when our church first used screens in our auditorium to display the sermon outlines, an occasional map or other graphic to help in preaching, and hymn lyrics. I was soundly rebuked by others who considered the use of screens worldly. It sounds silly now (especially since all of those who publicly criticized this step now use screens themselves), but it was disappointing and even discouraging to me at the time. Similarly, when we began using a platform ensemble to help lead the singing on Sunday mornings, some assumed we were copying churches with a rock band. In reality, we did it because we found having several singers on the platform encouraged greater participation in the congregational singing. We need to give grace to one another and, as an expression of biblical love, assume the best motives and intentions in outreach methods.

Just beware that in your desire for creativity you're not merely copying the over contextualization of others and claiming it as creativity or a new idea. Just because you employ a method that most independent Baptists don't use does not mean it is new or innovative. While thinking outside the box is helpful, it must be done within the biblical parameters of truth and holiness.

Biblical preaching is needed to reach our culture.

The New Testament tells us that God has chosen to use preaching as a primary tool in the proclamation of the gospel: "For after that in the wisdom of God the world by wisdom knew not God, it pleased God by the foolishness of preaching to save them that believe" (1 Corinthians 1:21).

In a day when preaching is looked down upon and often set aside in favor of more culturally-relatable methods, we must remember that preaching is not an option for a biblical church. It is part of the basic function of the church. The Greek word for *preach* is *kerusso* which means "to herald, as a public crier, to proclaim." Preaching, by nature, is to be an authoritative declaration of God's Word. Biblical preaching must be Spirit-filled, rightly dividing truth, and Christ-centered. But it must happen.

While Paul on Mars Hill understood and made references to the culture, he made bold declarations of the gospel. And, lest you think that preaching can be done such as to never offend the unsaved man, remember that Paul was ridiculed for his message.

> Then Paul stood in the midst of Mars' hill, and said, Ye men of Athens, I perceive that in all things ye are too superstitious. For as I passed by, and beheld your devotions, I found an altar with this inscription, TO THE UNKNOWN GOD. Whom therefore ye ignorantly worship, him declare I unto you. . . . For in him we live, and move, and have our being; as certain also of your own poets have said, For we are also his offspring . . . And when they heard of the resurrection of the dead, some mocked: and others said, We will hear thee again of this matter.
> —ACTS 17:22-23, 28, 32

Furthermore, Paul's awareness of culture did not preclude his preaching against certain aspects of it. He certainly did not include only the gospel, but preached against sins of the heart, body, and culture, as we see throughout the New Testament epistles. Just as in New Testament times, we often have unsaved people present in our church services (1 Corinthians 14:23–25). While we should be aware of their presence and faithful to deliver the gospel message, we must also faithfully expound God's Word, which includes preaching against the actual sins of our day as they are addressed in Scripture.

We must make pleasing Christ our target.

Man pleasing is such a deceitful temptation that it lands people in both ditches of the contextualization highway. The reality is that whether one cares about what the friends in their "fellowship" think or about what the world thinks, both the separatist and non-separatist have the same issue, and it is a dangerous one.

The Pharisees were guilty of man pleasing: "for they loved the praise of men more than the praise of God" (John 12:43). And the Galatians fell into it as well: "For do I now persuade men, or God? or do I seek to please men? for if I yet pleased men, I should not be the servant of Christ" (Galatians 1:10).

We must make Christ our target and Scripture our guide. We will answer to Him—not to one another—for faithfulness in our calling and to the truth which He has entrusted to our care. "Let a man so account of us, as of the ministers of Christ, and stewards of the mysteries of God. Moreover it is required in stewards, that a man be found faithful" (1 Corinthians 4:1–2).

CHAPTER EIGHT

MISSIONAL TRENDS

THERE IS NO QUESTION in my mind that the Great Commission of Christ comprises *the* mission statement of the local church:

> And Jesus came and spake unto them, saying, All power is given unto me in heaven and in earth. Go ye therefore, and teach all nations, baptizing them in the name of the Father, and of the Son, and of the Holy Ghost: Teaching them to observe all things whatsoever I have commanded you: and, lo, I am with you alway, even unto the end of the world. Amen.
> —MATTHEW 28:18–20

This mission should compel us, challenge us, motivate us, and, coupled with a love for Christ, *consume* us.

Like so many others past and present, I've given my life to obeying this commission and encouraging others to do the same. I preach the gospel and witness to the lost. I train, encourage, and organize opportunities for our church family to saturate our community with the gospel. I've invested much of my life in training ministerial students at West Coast Baptist College to proclaim the gospel. I've written books to encourage and equip Christians to share their faith. In short, I believe in the importance of the Great Commission and am constantly endeavoring to fully engage in it. And I believe that all Christians, regardless of their vocation, should give their lives to this great mission.

It is in this context that some leaders use the term *missional*. By it, they mean that sharing the gospel should be our life-wide mission—not merely something relegated to organized church outreach. I, too, believe we should be consumed with sharing the gospel in every facet of life, including purposeful community engagement with the intention of creating opportunities to share the gospel.

When, however, the term *missional* is used as the description of a primary ministry philosophy that discourages organized outreach in favor of only "organic" approaches to sharing the gospel, I am concerned. Some proponents even look at planned evangelism or soulwinning as anti-missional. This philosophy has created churches with less organization in the kind of evangelistic efforts that seek to saturate a community with the gospel and do not encourage members to purposefully schedule times for personal soulwinning.

Challenging people to be active in the community is good. From joining soccer leagues to supporting crisis pregnancy centers to hosting police officer barbecues to providing oil changes for single moms, our church family works to reach into our community with care, appreciation, and the love of Christ.

Encouraging people to see themselves as ambassadors for Christ throughout every aspect of their lives is good. I often remind our church family that the primary vocation of a Christian is not simply to be an engineer, nurse, teacher, janitor, or any other profession; but their mission is to be a Christian engineer who carries the gospel to work, a Christian nurse who has been entrusted with the gospel, etc.

But if we see our community engagement and normally-established relationships as our *only* platforms to share our faith, we will miss opportunities to proactively witness for Christ. Our church has seen over five hundred people baptized annually for over twenty years. This has been the work of the Holy Spirit empowering our church family as gospel witnesses. Some of these souls have been family members, coworkers, soccer coaches, and fellow students saved through the witness of our church family. But many have been initially reached through door-to-door outreach or large scale evangelistic events, such as an Open House Sunday or Easter presentation where the gospel was preached. So, while it is important for us as Christians to live *missional* lives that are structured around sharing the gospel, for a church to consider that its primary gospel strategy may be shortsighted.

We need both spontaneous ministry and strategically-organized ministry. We need people who will share the gospel with their coworkers, explain their transformed lives to their families, *and* specifically reach out to people they would otherwise never talk to in order to share the gospel. And, because the Great Commission is Christ's mission to the local church, I believe that, just as church leaders should provide structure in reaching the world through a church's mission program, they should provide structure for engaging the church family in saturating their community with the gospel.

TERMS AND ORIGINS

Although Baptists today have picked up the terms *missional* or *gospel-centered* from contemporary leaders, such as Timothy Keller or D. A.

Carson, the philosophies behind the terms trace back further. In large part, these philosophies were promoted by the names we'll look at in this section, which Keller, Carson, and others often quote. The men listed below were used by God, but they had concerning doctrinal views, of which you should be aware.

John Stott—He was a masterful writer with an ability to craft strong gospel quotes, which I occasionally use. But he was also an Anglican priest, believed annihilationism was a real possibility, and taught (including at the Lausanne Conference in 1974) that social action must be a part of the gospel.[1]

Karl Barth—One of the leading theologians of the twentieth century, Barth taught, not that Scripture has been inspired as a completed action of God, but that Scripture becomes the inspired Word of God when received by a believer.[2] Because he rejected the extreme liberalism of German rationalism, some have considered him conservative. But in truth, he was neo-orthodox; he rejected biblical inerrancy and questioned various aspects of the Bible's accuracy.[3]

Lesslie Newbigin—A British theologian who served many years as a missionary in India, Newbigin's work laid the foundation for the modern missional church movement. He is remembered for his insistence on confronting Western, secularized culture with the gospel. And yet, he was a strong ecumenicist and for several years served as the associate general

---

1   Alister Chapman, *Godly Ambition: John Stott and the Evangelical* (New York: Oxford University Press, 2012), 139–140, 145. See also Stott's comments including his arguments that "the ultimate annihilation of the wicked should at least be accepted as a legitimate, biblically founded alternative to their eternal conscious torment." Robert A. Peterson, *Hell on Trial: The Case for Eternal Punishment* (Phillipsburg: Presbyterian & Reformed Publishing, 1995), 320.

2   John Morrison, "Barth, Barthinians, and Evangelicals: Reassessing the Question of the Relation of Holy Scripture and the Word of God," *Trinity Journal* 25, no. 2 (September 1, 2004): 197-98.

3   Karl Barth, *Church Dogmatics*, Vol. 1.2, Study Edition 5 (London: T & T Clark, 2010), 510.

secretary of the World Council of Churches (WCC).[4] (A recent article on The Gospel Coalition website specifically encouraged pastors to read more of Lesslie Newbigin's writings.)[5]

Carl Henry—The founding academic dean of Fuller Theological Seminary, Henry was one of the early champions of the New Evangelical movement.[6] He was conservative in his doctrine but wrote and spoke out against fundamentalism and its practice of separation from apostasy.[7] He was instrumental in launching the ecumenical National Association of Evangelicals (NAE) and was the founding editor of the liberal-leaning magazine, *Christianity Today*.[8]

I don't list these names to censure these men, but to raise your awareness of their larger perspective and to challenge you to be discerning as you consider their influence on modern ministry trends. As you read people who quote them, it's important that you read from the vantage point of knowing their views. These, and others, invested great energy in their quest to blend fundamental men with the theological liberals of their day. They wanted unity at all costs and felt that if Christians would prioritize social needs, they should be able to concede their liberal or conservative biases toward doctrine for the greater good. Reading an author who extensively quotes these men, or others with similar emphases, helps one understand the foundation of and thus direction a particular trend is heading.

---

4   Gerald H. Anderson, ed., *Biographical Dictionary of Christian Missions* (Grand Rapids: Wm. B. Eerdmans Publishing, 1999), 491.
5   Nathan Finn, "Why Pastors Should Read Lesslie Newbigin," *The Gospel Coalition*, February 25, 2019, https://www.thegospelcoalition.org/reviews/church-vocation.
6   "Henry's Story," *Carl F. Henry Institute for Cultural Engagement*, accessed November 8, 2019, https://henryinstitute.org/henrys-story.
7   See in particular his book *The Uneasy Conscience of Modern Fundamentalism* (Grand Rapids: Wm. B. Eerdmans Publishing, 1947).
8   "Henry's Story."

DILUTING THE GOSPEL

Practiced according to its strongest proponents, *missional* is much like the *lifestyle evangelism* of the 1980s. The idea behind lifestyle evangelism was that you would live in such a way that others would see your faith and ask you questions that would lead to gospel conversations. Indeed, 1 Peter 3:15 instructs us, "But sanctify the Lord God in your hearts: and be ready always to give an answer to every man that asketh you a reason of the hope that is in you with meekness and fear." If we are living godly lives in the midst of unsaved people, there will be opportunities to answer questions that lead to sharing the gospel.

But—and this is important—living a godly life is not the same as sharing the gospel. In fact, it's not really evangelism at all until the gospel is actually shared. The Bible tells us, "So then faith cometh by hearing, and hearing by the word of God" (Romans 10:17).

The weakness of lifestyle evangelism was not in its encouragement to live out the gospel in daily life; its weakness was in calling daily living "evangelism." I see a similar weakness with the common understanding of missional living. Proponents encourage the purposeful development of relationships with lost people, pointing to Christ who was a "friend of publicans and sinners" (Luke 7:34) and contrasting that with many Christians whose entire social life revolves around the church. I agree to a point. We *should* develop relationships with lost people— neighbors, coworkers, and even those outside of our normal realms of interaction. But having a relationship is not the same as sharing the gospel. And having a relationship is not a *prerequisite* for sharing the gospel. When we forget either of those two truths, we become timid in sharing our faith—either substituting kind thoughts and prayers for our gospel witness, or believing it's just not quite time yet to confront someone with their need for a Savior.

Furthermore, if a relationship is required to share the gospel, what about the hundreds of thousands of people in our cities with whom we can't nurture a personal relationship? Should we not find ways to saturate entire communities with the gospel, as Paul did? Paul would go into a foreign city and immediately begin engaging people with the gospel— whether that was in the synagogue, market place, or some other publicly available forum. (See Acts 13:5, 15, 42; 14:1; 16:13; 17:17; and 20:20.)

The idea that sharing the gospel should only be pursued through individual relationships sets up an either/or, rather than a both/and proposition. Should we love our neighbors and be active members of our communities? Yes! Should we build relationships for the sake of the gospel? Of course! Should we care for the fatherless, poor, and neglected? Absolutely! But does that mean we can *only* share the gospel in these settings with these people after we have first proved to them our love? Not at all.

In an interview as the then-new SBC president, J. D. Greear stated, "Our preaching of the gospel must be accompanied by acts of extravagant gospel generosity."[9] Indeed, we are to love our neighbors, and we are to be generous people. But if we create a self-imposed requirement that we must give to the poor or help the marginalized in every case that we preach the gospel, we will either preach it less or become timid in sharing our faith.

Author Rodman MacIlvaine suggested a similar idea in his article "What Is the Missional Church Movement?" He wrote, "Missional Christians generally display common ground with the world, first through generous acts of service but also through the arts and at times

---

9   Justin Taylor, "A Conversation with J. D. Greear, the New President of the Southern Baptist Convention," *The Gospel Coalition*, June 12, 2018, https://www. thegospelcoalition.org/blogs/justintaylorj-d-greear-elected-as-the-62nd-president-of-the-southern-baptistconvention.

through positions of leadership within the community or state. *Having earned the right to be heard . . ."*[10] (emphasis mine). While there may be some who will not hear us until we show them the love of Christ, our primary calling is not to earn a right to be heard. The command of Christ is our mandate. He has given us the responsibility to proclaim the gospel "to *every* creature" (Mark 16:15).

Author Timothy Keller, in his church philosophy book *Center Church,* agrees that there are various types of "missional churches," including many that have lost the gospel emphasis. Unfortunately, Keller insists, "Ministry in which Christians sacrificially serve the common good of the city is not only biblical but a necessary context for any convincing call to believe in Jesus."[11] In other words, if we are not intentionally serving, we haven't "earned the right to be heard." While I believe we must serve our community, and we have done so in various ways for decades, we must share the gospel with those we may not know or have had an opportunity to serve.

Keller, however, says that we cannot change culture simply "through lots of conversions."[12] I disagree. Scripture teaches that the truly converted become "a new creature" (2 Corinthians 5:17). As someone grows in their faith, everything about their life will change, including developing biblical viewpoints on moral and social issues. Those who insist that a missional, gospel-centered model must focus on social justice can sometimes do the gospel itself an injustice by seemingly suggesting that conversion is not the answer.

---

10 Rodman MacIlvaine, "What Is the Missional Church Movement?," *Bibliotheca Sacra* 167:665 (January 2010), 92.
11 Timothy Keller, *Center Church: Doing Balanced, Gospel-Centered Ministry in Your City* (Grand Rapids, MI: Zondervan, 2012), 291.
12 Ibid.

In fact, a related concern to me of the missional movement is its emphasis on the social gospel and social justice (which we'll look at more fully in chapter 9). But Keller describes a gospel-centered model as a church where "conversion, deep Christian community, social justice, and cultural renewal in the city" are philosophical pillars.[13] (If "cultural renewal in the city" is a model of what success looks like, then I know of few, if any, truly successful churches today.) Tobi England, one of the Bible instructors at West Coast Baptist College, recently offered an insightful and concise observation: "Missional philosophy can have some good attributes, like the desire to see people saved. However, it often is a mile wide and an inch deep. By expanding God's mission to all social ills (e.g. social justice, AIDs, environmentalism), it dilutes or neglects the singular purpose for missions which is making disciples (Matthew 28:19)."[14]

Some proponents of the missional movement point to their focus on social causes by suggesting that, since social ills point back to the fall and the break of our relationship with God, part of a restored relationship with God is restoring the benefits lost through the fall. In the book *Missional Renaissance*, Reggie McNeal suggests this very thing:

[God] wants to restore not just the nature of his intended relationship with people but the benefits of it as well. Adequate food, restorative rest, authentic relationships, life in harmony with the rest of the created order ... these are blessings that God granted in the Garden and still wants humanity to experience. ... He declared that he had come to give life, life to the full. This means that missional Jesus

---

13 Ibid.
14 Tobi England, M. Div. Instructor, West Coast Baptist College, personal correspondence with the author.

> followers are engaged in all aspects of human experience—political,
> social, economic, cultural, physical, psychological, and spiritual . . . [15]

This way of thinking has little support from the New Testament. Although Jesus did combine spiritual teaching and preaching with physical acts of kindness, these were mainly miracles (which are outside of our ability) intended to validate His teaching and divinity (Acts 2:22). They were certainly not a direct aspect of the Great Commission, or even implied in it.

Whatever involvement churches have in social ills, they cannot allow this to be a substitute for sharing the gospel itself. For example, our church financially supports both a local rescue mission and a crisis pregnancy center. But this is no replacement for telling these same people of their need for the riches found in Christ alone. Physical needs are important. But if we don't take the gospel to our communities, we become just another civic organization. When I was a missionary kid in Korea, we often helped the homeless and gave the gospel as we did so. Even today, when I have the opportunity to preach in Central American schools, we have brought sports equipment and perhaps played sports with the students and then preached the gospel.

Here in our community, I regularly nurture relationships with lost people, praying for an opportunity to specifically share the gospel with them. Through this, I've had the opportunity to lead neighbors, businessmen, and community leaders to Christ. Additionally, I regularly go door-to-door in our city to engage people in one-on-one conversations about the gospel. And I see fruit from this as well. And then our church regularly hosts evangelistic events. We also see fruit from these. (In fact, many of our members have seen these events as great opportunities to

---

15   Reggie McNeal, *Missional Renaissance: Changing the Scorecard for the Church* (San Francisco, CA: Jossey-Bass, 2009), 35.

invite an unsaved person with whom they already have a relationship to come hear the gospel preached.) Some refer to this as "attractional ministry." I don't care what one calls it, but the fact is there is no ministry when the Word of God is not shared.

Although many seem to call practically everything *ministry*, most usages of the word in the New Testament were in the context of aiding in or teaching of the Word of God. (See Acts 6:4, 20:24, 21:19, and Ephesians 4:11–12.) Just because an act of service is performed by someone who happens to be a Christian or has a kind intention, doesn't make it ministry. If real life change will take place, it will be through the powerful Word of God and specifically through the gospel of Christ. For something to be ministry, the imparting of God's Word must be included. But for those with a missional philosophy, the priority is developing relationships in which they hope, over time, to share the gospel.

Why should we say that relationships alone should be the priority—even if that means fewer opportunities to share the gospel on a broader scale? And lest you think I'm exaggerating, this is what authors Tim Chester and Steve Timmis suggested in their book *Total Church:* "Being both gospel-centered and community-centered might mean . . . running fewer evangelistic events, youth clubs, and social projects and spending more time sharing our lives with unbelievers."[16] Ed Stetzer also acknowledged in an interview with *Biola Magazine* titled "Inside the Missional Movement" that, yes, there may be fewer converts in a missional church (although he did say the church shouldn't defend its lack of converts).[17]

If we must earn a right to be heard, we won't share the gospel as often. And if we think our testimony alone will draw people to Christ, we won't

---

16   Tim Chester and Steve Timmis, *Total Church: A Radical Reshaping Around Gospel and Community* (Wheaton, IL: Crossway Books, 2008), 18.
17   "Inside the Missional Movement: An Exclusive Interview with Ed Stetzer," *Biola Magazine,* accessed October 14, 2019, http://magazine.biola.edu/article/09-spring/inside-the-missional-movement.

share the actual gospel at all. May I suggest that we return to keeping the direct proclamation of the gospel as our focus?

GETTING THE GOSPEL RIGHT

I think one reason missional ministry has become so attractive is because of concern about massive outreach efforts that have sometimes resulted in little lasting fruit. Millennial leaders, disillusioned with reports of thousands of people saved through mass outreach but little to no measurable change in a local church body, are rethinking how to reach people with the gospel. For a generation who values authenticity and community, something as organic as building relationships is not only appealing, but it feels right.

I sympathize with this reasoning. If the choice is between massive false professions of faith and slow, hard-won relationships resulting in a few professions of faith with changed lives, I would take the second option as well.

But I don't believe those are the choices. In fact, if you study the book of Acts, you see that the Lord greatly blessed the early church and the apostle Paul in both large-scale and personal conversation evangelism efforts. Sometimes Paul's fruit was the result of sharing the gospel with someone with whom he already had a relationship; however, most often it was a proclamation made to a complete stranger.

Although there are many dynamics involved in the response to the gospel from people in different fields of ministry, I think there are a few reasons that some large-scale efforts have failed to yield lasting fruit:

Unclear gospel presentations—A simplistic gospel presentation that allows mere mental agreement with the generalities of the gospel—*Sure, I've done bad things and am willing to say your prayer to go to Heaven*—

doesn't result in a regenerated life. Repeating a prayer is not receiving God's gift of salvation; turning to Christ in repentance and faith is (Acts 20:21). If the gospel presentation is inaccurate or unclear to the unsaved hearer, we can hardly expect fruit that remains, no matter how large the initial response of "decisions" may be. (Incidentally, unclear gospel presentations happen in many types of ministry models, such as invitations with the general suggestion to "turn your life over to God.")

Those of us who lead churches in a soulwinning emphasis must be careful that we are clearly presenting the gospel and teaching others to do the same. New Testament soulwinning relies on the Holy Spirit to bring conviction and draw a hearer to Christ, and it depends on someone clearly sharing the death, burial, and resurrection of Christ for our sins (1 Corinthians 15:1–4).

Lack of follow up—A new Christian needs a tremendous amount of spiritual nurturing. This is an area in which the apostle Paul excelled (1 Thessalonians 2), and that is obvious in the churches that the Lord used him to establish throughout his missionary journeys.

When you consider how Paul was sometimes only in a new city for a matter of months, it's obvious that he wasn't taking long periods of time to earn a community's trust before he would present the gospel. In fact, the long-term relationships that Paul nurtured were generally on the discipleship end of his ministry. Paul was willing to spend and be spent for those he led to Christ, even when they weren't showing much spiritual growth (2 Corinthians 12:15). I doubt the first century churches Paul planted would have flourished without this kind of labor from Paul, no matter how many people came to Christ during Paul's initial ministry in that city.

In our church, consistent follow up on new converts and intentional discipleship have had a significant impact on the attrition rate of new

Christians.[18] Without acceptance, instruction, and involvement, a newly saved Christian may very easily fall back into an old lifestyle. For these reasons, we work to create a culture of spiritual nurturing in our church family, and especially in our adult Bible classes.

Over programming and under depending—One other weakness of soulwinning-focused churches that I believe has encouraged some to turn toward a missional model is over programming ministry while at the same time not emphasizing dependence on the Holy Spirit.

I believe that churches should have organized outreach efforts and encourage Christians to schedule time specifically to engage people with the gospel. This allows a church to intentionally reach into every sector of their community with the gospel and helps Christians to intentionally engage in the Great Commission. The danger, however, is when we send the signal that the *only* time to share the gospel is Saturday mornings at 9:30 when you are carrying a handful of gospel tracts and have a partner. The reality is that we should be on mission with the gospel everywhere we go. We are ambassadors for Christ and stand in His stead with everyone to whom we speak. Furthermore, without the work of the Holy Spirit, our best efforts can never reach a soul.

FAITH COMES BY HEARING

When it comes to gospel focus, we must remember that Scripture directly tells us how people come to trust Christ: "So then faith cometh by hearing, and hearing by the word of God" (Romans 10:17). It is the specific sharing of the gospel that must take place for people to trust Christ.

---

18   We use the book *Continue* (Lancaster, CA: Striving Together Publications, 2015) for our organized discipleship program.

The gospel has incredible power to change lives . . . if we will simply share it. In fact, when we consider the Great Commission of Christ, there is nothing greater, nothing more pressing, nothing more constraining than this mission given to us by God to go into all the world and preach the gospel.

So, should we be missional? Yes! Our entire lives should be wrapped around the mission Christ gave to us. But should being missional constrain us from personally, passionately, and persistently sharing the gospel? God forbid.

May we who have been entrusted with the gospel as ambassadors of Christ be faithful to deliver His message.

CHAPTER NINE

SOCIAL JUSTICE TRENDS

Some of the most moving biographies I have read have been of people who lived out James 1:27 in profound and life-altering ways: "Pure religion and undefiled before God and the Father is this, To visit the fatherless and widows in their affliction, and to keep himself unspotted from the world."

I have studied the lives of people like George Müller who rescued, housed, fed, and educated ten thousand orphans from the streets of England; Amy Carmichael who spent fifty years in India rescuing young girls from a life of temple prostitution; and William Wilberforce who labored tirelessly in the British Parliament to see slavery outlawed. I think these are the kinds of people and needs that conservative Christians often have in mind when they hear the term *social justice*. Scripture calls us to live compassionately and give generously. All throughout the Old Testament, God commanded His people to care for the poor, the foreigner, and the outcast. (See Deuteronomy 10:18, Psalm 140:12, Ezekiel 22:29.)

Justice is a Bible word, and *injustice* is repeatedly censured as sin in Scripture. God is a just God, and He specifically commands us to "do justly": "He hath shewed thee, O man, what is good; and what doth the Lord require of thee, but to do justly, and to love mercy, and to walk humbly with thy God?" (Micah 6:8).

Likewise, there are other sins that social justice proponents point to which the Bible does condemn. For instance, greed is a sin. First Timothy 6:6–10 warns of the danger to one's soul through the goal of riches, of loving money, and of coveting.

Racism is also a sin. God made every person in His image (Genesis 1:27), and we all have equal value in His sight. Acts 17:25–26 tells us, "He giveth to all life, and breath, and all things; And hath made of one blood all nations of men." Treating anyone as inferior because of their skin color or ethnicity is abhorrent to God. We are all one race—the human race.

Similar to racism, partiality is also sin. James 2 specifically condemns treating people differently based on their social standing or perceived benefit to us. In fact, the Bible warns against partiality in *any* direction—favoring either the poor or the well-connected: "Ye shall do no unrighteousness in judgment: thou shalt not respect the person of the poor, nor honour the person of the mighty: but in righteousness shalt thou judge thy neighbour" (Leviticus 19:15).

So as we enter this discussion on social justice, I want to emphasize that God calls us to be people of both justice and compassion. Love—perhaps the unifying capstone of both of these virtues—is to be an identifying mark of Christians: "By this shall all men know that ye are my disciples, if ye have love one to another" (John 13:35).

If there is *anyone* who should care about and care for the needy, outcast, foreigner, and downtrodden, it should be Christians. We serve a God who created, loves, and has mercy on all people. Our biblical doctrine should not only dictate our position; it should also dictate our personal values and call us to lives of sacrificial generosity and service.

Christians and local churches should be involved in their communities and be concerned for justice. They should stand with those who are mistreated, and they should serve those who are in need. In fact, the New Testament repeatedly emphasizes the importance of our doing good works. We were created by God to do them (Ephesians 2:10), they adorn the gospel message (1 Timothy 2:10), they should accompany any wealth God gives to us (1 Timothy 6:18), they are part of Christian discipleship (Titus 2:7), and a zeal to do them should characterize the life of every believer (Titus 2:14).

But I think it is also important that we understand the larger picture of the social justice movement, because what I just described is not what is commonly understood by *social justice* in the secular world. In fact, social justice has decidedly anti-Christian roots. As I see well-meaning Christians jump on its bandwagon in the name of furthering the gospel, I am troubled because the social justice movement is headed a direction that is very much away from the truth.

This chapter is not an exhaustive study of all social justice issues, although we'll look at a handful of instances for sake of example. But primarily, I want us to step back and get a big-picture look at the definition, origin, and direction of the social justice movement, while emphasizing how that relates to gospel ministry.

WHAT IS SOCIAL JUSTICE?

Part of what is challenging about these discussions is that *social justice* is a fluid term that means different things to different people. But the widely-understood secular meaning includes a belief that wealth and privilege should be redistributed from those who have received much and be given to those who have been disadvantaged. And usually the determination of privilege or disadvantage is determined based on group identity rather than the opportunity or need of individuals.

If this sounds extreme to you, allow me to provide a couple definitions from credible sources:

The exact definition in the online *Oxford Dictionary* for *social justice* is "justice in terms of the distribution of wealth, opportunities, and privileges within a society." It then provides the example sentence: "Individuality gives way to the struggle for social justice."[1]

Author and scholar William H. Young explains, "While often an amorphous term, 'social justice' has evolved to generally mean state redistribution of advantages and resources to disadvantaged groups to satisfy their rights to social and economic equality."[2]

There is no question that the secular view of social justice has roots of Marxism and racism and a goal toward socialism.[3] What is debated among Christians, however, is to what extent the term *social justice* can or should be used to support causes of Christlike compassion versus to what extent using and identifying with the term aids unrighteous causes.

John MacArthur, who has taken a strong position against using the term in gospel ministry wrote,

---

1   *Lexico*, s.v. "social justice," accessed October 18, 2019, https://www.lexico.com/en/definition/social_justice.

2   William H. Young, "Academic Social Science and Social Justice," *National Association of Scholars*, August 28, 2015, https://www.nas.org/blogs/dicta/academic_social_science_and_social_justice.

3   Stephen Thomas Kirschner, "Cultural Marxism: The origins of the present day social justice movement, and political correctness," *The Policy*, February 14, 2017, https://thepolicy.us/cultural-marxism-the-origins-of-the-present-day-social-justice-movement-and-political-correctness-ffb89c6ef4f1. See also Michael Novak, "Social Justice: Not What You Think It Is," *The Heritage Foundation*, December 29, 2009, https://www.heritage.org/poverty-and-inequality/report/social-justice-not-what-you-think-it. Also see Claudio Corradetti, "The Frankfurt School and Critical Theory," *Internet Encyclopedia of Philosophy*, Accessed June 10, 2020, https://www.iep.utm.edu/frankfur/#H3.

"Social justice" (in the world's usage of that term) entails political ideas that are deemed sophisticated—namely, identity politics, critical race theory, the redistribution of wealth, and other radical or socialist policies. Those ideas were first popularized and propagated in the secular academy, where they are now regarded as received wisdom and have become a dominating part of popular culture. Evangelicals who are chasing the culture are latecomers to the party of those who advocate "social justice."[4]

MacArthur brings up some terms here to which we can only give a cursory glance. If you study these terms further, however, you will find that he is correct. The definitions below are from *Oxford Dictionary* and *Encyclopedia Britannica:*

- *Identity Politics*—"A tendency for people of a particular religion, race, social background, etc., to form exclusive political alliances, moving away from traditional broad-based party politics."[5]
- *Critical Race Theory (CRT)*—the view that race, instead of being biologically grounded and natural, is socially constructed and that race, as a socially constructed concept, functions as a means to maintain the interests of the white population that constructed it. According to CRT, racial inequality emerges from the social, economic, and legal differences that white people create between "races" to maintain elite white interest in labour markets and politics and as such create the circumstances that give rise to poverty and criminality in many minority communities.[6]

---

4   John MacArthur, "The Long Struggle to Preserve the Gospel, Part 2," *Grace to You*, August 22, 2018, https://www.gty.org/library/blog/B180822.

5   *Lexico*, s.v. "identity politics," accessed October 18, 2019, https://www.lexico.com/en/definition/identity_politics.

6   Tommy Curry, "Critical Race Theory," *Encyclopaedia Britannica*, accessed October 18, 2019, https://www.britannica.com/topic/critical-race-theory

- *Intersectionality*—The interconnected nature of social categorizations such as race, class, and gender as they apply to a given individual or group, regarded as creating overlapping and interdependent systems of discrimination or disadvantage.[7]

These ideas are antithetical to the gospel, which is why many of us were concerned to see the Southern Baptist Convention pass a resolution in June 2019 to use CRT and intersectionality as analytic tools.[8] I have deep concerns about how well we represent the truth of the gospel when we, in an effort to be more compassionate and sensitive, turn to the world for its analysis of both problems and their answers. In the case of the terms just given, the world has both the problem and the answer wrong.

SOCIAL JUSTICE AND ITS RADICAL AGENDA

The socialistic agenda behind social justice is what prompted the economist and Nobel Prize winner Friedrich Hayek to write, "I have come to feel strongly that the greatest service I can still render to my fellow men would be that I could make the speakers and writers among them thoroughly ashamed ever again to employ the term 'social justice.'"[9] In an online article, author Jonah Goldberg writes that from an economic standpoint,

---

7   *Lexico*, s.v. "intersectionality," accessed October 18, 2019, https://www.lexico.com/en/definition/intersectionality.

8   "On Critical Race Theory and Intersectionality," *Southern Baptist Convention*, accessed October 18, 2019, http://www.sbc.net/resolutions/2308/resolution-9--on-critical-race-theory-and-intersectionality. Albert Mohler also raised concerns with this resolution on his podcast. The transcript is worth a read: Albert Mohler, "Ideas Have Consequences: Critical Race Theory and Intersectionality in the News from the Southern Baptist Convention," *Albert Mohler*, June 14, 2019, https://albertmohler.com/2019/06/14/briefing-6-14-19.

9   F. A. Hayek, *Law, Legislation and Liberty, Volume 2: The Mirage of Social Justice* (Chicago, IL: University of Chicago Press, 1976), 97.

[Hayek] understood that beneath the political opportunism and intellectual laziness of the term "social justice" was a pernicious philosophical claim, namely that freedom must be sacrificed in order to redistribute income. Ultimately, "social justice" is about the state amassing ever increasing power in order to do "good things." What are good things? Well whatever the champions of social justice decide this week. But first, last and always it is the cause of economic redistribution.[10]

To me, however, the issue is far greater than an economic one. It has become an issue in which American Christians, under the banner of love and compassion, have capitulated to the demands of a godless culture.

For sake of example, consider the group called Faithful America. Their website explains, "We are the largest online community of Christians putting faith into action for social justice."[11] The same web page lists some of their successes:

- Fought back against Hobby Lobby
- Convinced Google to drop World Vision
- Forced MSNBC to drop the Family Research Council
- Helped students win justice for fired principal (This was a vice principle who was fired from a Catholic high school because he was gay.)
- Defended an unjustly-defrocked pastor (This was a Methodist pastor who, against the orders of his denomination, officiated a same-sex wedding for his son.)

Does this sound like a Christian agenda?

10   Jonah Goldberg, "What Is Social Justice?," *PragerU,* accessed October 18, 2019, https://www.prageru.com/sites/default/files/courses/transcripts/goldberg-what_is_ social_justice-transcript.pdf.
11   *Faithful America,* accessed October 17, 2019, https://act.faithfulamerica.org/signup/ about-us.

It's easy for Bible-believing Christians to look at a group like that and say, "That's not at all what *we* want when we advocate for social justice." But I don't think it's so easy to use the term *social justice* and expect that the world will understand that you mean something different by it.

The fact is that the secular social justice movement not only begins with a Marxist, socialist bias to economic issues and civil rights, but it seeks to hitch feminism and LGBTQ rights to the same bias. The end goal is that being against same-sex marriage will be seen by the general populace as being equivalent to being a member of the Ku Klux Klan.[12]

So how does this radical agenda affect Bible-believing, Baptist pastors? In a willingness to reconsider biblical doctrine in light of worldly philosophy, I am watching Bible-believing Christians weaken their stand on some of the very issues promoted by the social justice movement—such as same-sex marriage.

A sad example of where this leads was apparent in a 2016 tweet by Bill Hybels, one of the original leaders of the seeker-sensitive movement (who has since resigned his church amidst various allegations). In response to the horrific shooting in an Orlando gay nightclub, he posted, "Our family mourns with all those grieving in Orlando, and with our LGBT brothers and sisters everywhere."[13] I also grieved for the lives lost in that shooting and the loved ones whose hearts were broken by it. I prayed that people would come to Christ through this tragic event. But referring to those in unrepentant, sinful lifestyles as "brothers and sisters" is not scriptural and doesn't help lead people to Christ.

---

12 This is a point that Voddie Baucham brought out in a sermon critiquing the social justice movement. In his message, he presented three main areas that secular social justice seeks to advance: minority equality, feminism and women's rights, and LGBTQ rights. The message is available on YouTube at https://youtu.be/YFNOP2IqwoY.

13 Bill Hybels, Twitter post, June 13, 2016, https://twitter.com/BillHybels.

More recently, another pastor told his congregation that "we should whisper about what the Bible whispers about and shout about what it shouts about. The Bible appears more to whisper on sexual sin compared to its shouts about materialism and religious pride."[14] The pastor who said this professes to still believe same-sex marriage is wrong. But statements such as these do not make Christians seem more compassionate (as the goal may have been); they reveal a weakening stand.

The other way in which the social justice movement affects Bible-believing pastors is in its tendency to create a pendulum swing. For instance, relative to the quote just given, there have been times in which pastors have said ugly, hateful things directed toward homosexuals or about same-sex marriage. Sadly, these types of statements have further alienated some people who have been vulnerable to the sin of homosexuality. The answer to this problem, however, is not to swing the pendulum the other direction and make vague statements that suggest our sexuality is not an issue according to the Bible. The answer is to take a firm, biblical position while preaching the truth in love. Again, when we allow the world to define both the problem and the answer, we will respond unbiblically. In this area, the world defines the problem as hate and the answer as acceptance. The real problem is sin, and the answer is Jesus.

Another area in which some Christian leaders are succumbing to the agenda of social justice is the area of the biblical roles for men and women in the home and church. Here in America, we're in the midst of a backlash toward sexual assault and abuse. Victims and advocates for victims have identified themselves with the #metoo hashtag. I am unequivocally against any kind of sexual assault or abuse and am especially grieved when the

---

14   J. D. Greear, "How the Fall Affects Us All" YouTube video, 1:29:53, posted by "The Summit Church," January 27, 2019, https://youtu.be/6mjRcqvXppM.

perpetrator is a Christian, when it goes unreported, or when Christians offer anything less than support and help toward healing for victims.[15]

But in the midst of this backlash, I'm concerned that Bible-believing Christians are failing to distinguish the undertones of rejection for God's designed roles for men and women. Rather than recognizing the nuances of philosophy embedded in these discussions, many Christians are taking up a cause that tends to equate all male leadership with abuse and all philosophies of feminism as a repressed champion. Consequently, even in churches, I'm seeing a strong moving toward egalitarianism—the belief that since men and women are equal, their roles should be indistinguishable.

What we need to remember is that where there is a real problem in culture, the world's solution creates new difficulties. As followers of Christ, we have superior answers, and those answers are ultimately found in *the* superior answer of the gospel. Thus, while we should listen to and help hurting people who raise concerns of injustice, we should be aware that solutions based in worldly wisdom will not bring ultimate healing. Instead, we should seek godly wisdom and discernment to understand where there is imbalance or sin and bring biblical truth to correct it.

The biblical center between the two ungodly polar opposites of chauvinism and feminism is not egalitarianism, but complementarianism—that God made men and women equal in every sense and gave them differing roles in marriage (1 Peter 3:7) and in the church (1 Timothy 2:12). Although Scripture teaches that women are to submit to their own husbands (Ephesians 5:24), it also teaches that men are to sacrificially love their wives as Christ loved the church

---

15   I have written at length about this in *The Road Ahead* as well as on my blog. See, in particular, the post "Covering Abuse and Sin Is a Tragedy for the Work of Christ," December 12, 2018 (https://paulchappell.com/2018/12/12/covering-abuse-and-sin-is-a-tragedy-for-the-work-of-christ/), which also links to previous posts.

(Ephesians 5:25); and it does not teach that all women are to submit to all men. So yes, we must absolutely stand against abuse in any form. We must guard against male chauvinism and be willing to call it out. But we must not capitulate to an equally dangerous opposite extreme. If we do that, we simply follow the world rather than showing it a better way.

I believe that some churches promoting egalitarianism today will promote the gay agenda tomorrow. This is not because every egalitarian becomes a liberal, but because if the motive in becoming egalitarian is a pragmatic desire to be non-offensive to a world that has lost its way in respect to definitions of gender, marriage, and roles, we will continue to follow the world in ever-deepening distortions of truth.

The New Testament gives straightforward directions in 1 Timothy 2:12 and 1 Corinthians 14:35: "But I suffer not a woman to teach, nor to usurp authority over the man, but to be in silence." "And if they will learn any thing, let them ask their husbands at home: for it is a shame for women to speak in the church." Yet, seemingly in an attempt to please our culture, I'm watching Baptist leaders explain this verse away as they blur the lines of male pastoral leadership in preaching settings. Some seem to place more emphasis on women preachers than gospel preaching.

In the spring of 2019, a fire storm was ignited when Beth Moore announced that she would be bringing a message in a Southern Baptist Church on Mother's Day.[16] In response to an SBC seminary professor who wrote a blog calling Moore out and highlighting the complementarian order of Scripture, Moore doubled down. Rather than clarifying or more fully explaining what role her presence and words would play in that church service, she wrote a series of tweets in which she claimed that the Holy Spirit was calling her "to draw attention to the sexism & misogyny

---

16   Beth Moore, Twitter post, April 27, 2019, 6:45 a.m., https://twitter.com/bethmoorelpm.
      Beth Moore, Twitter post, May 9, 2019, 7:31 a.m., https://twitter.com/bethmoorelpm.

that is rampant in segments of the SBC, cloaked by piety & bearing the stench of hypocrisy."[17]

My wife Terrie is an avid student of God's Word and a capable Bible teacher. She has spoken to ladies over the years and has occasionally given a testimony of thanksgiving in our church assembly. But scripturally, neither she nor I believe it is a woman's place to teach or preach the Word of God in a mixed congregation.

In a fair and well-reasoned article on this subject, author Kevin DeYoung presents and interacts with complementation-based arguments for women preaching, specifically by those who make the case by distinguishing between the words "teaching, exhorting, evangelizing, prophesying, reading, and so on." DeYoung offers the following in the conclusion of his article:

> With all these elements of preaching jumbled together, how could Paul have expected Timothy to untangle the ball of yarn and know what he was supposed to not permit women to do? Just as importantly, how are we to discern when a sermon is just exhortation without authority and when it moves into an authoritative transmission of the apostolic deposit? Perhaps it would be better to see "teaching" as more or less what the preacher does on Sunday as opposed to a highly technical term that doesn't make sense out of the early church, the Jewish synagogue, Jesus's example, or Paul's instructions.
>
> The heraldic event—no matter the platform provided by the pastor or the covering given by the elders—cannot be separated from exercising authority and teaching, the two things women are not permitted do in the worship service.[18]

---

17 Beth Moore, Twitter post, May 11, 2019, 6:15 a.m., https://twitter.com/BethMooreLPM.
18 Kevin DeYoung, "Should Women Preach in Our Churches?," *The Gospel Coalition,* August 26, 2019, https://www.thegospelcoalition.org/blogs/kevin-deyoung/women-preach-churches.

We must be careful that we speak from God's Word to the issues of our culture rather than attempting to adjust Scripture to culture.

In his book *The Gathering Storm: Secularism, Culture and the Church,* author Albert Mohler gives an example of the radical nature of the social justice movement and how it can fundamentally change the very doctrinal moorings of the church. In fact, he describes how this exact thing happened to an entire denomination, the United Church of Canada, through a theological downgrade beginning in the 1960s. He concluded, "Social justice concerns propelled the denomination rather than theological commitments. As such, this church became a servant to secularism and liberalism in Canada. It pioneered transgender ministers, supported abortion, and championed same-sex marriage, even before it became legal in Canada."[19]

When culture becomes our gauge for what is offensive or helpful to the gospel, we will give an uncertain sound concerning truth, righteousness, and the Bible itself. The church will never please the world when it is living by the New Testament. Our goal must not be to appease an angry culture; it must be to please God and declare the gospel.

SOCIAL JUSTICE AND THE GOSPEL

Besides our stand on individual issues, a preoccupation with social issues can hijack our focus on the gospel.

The social justice movement of today, in fact, reaches back to the social gospel movement of the early twentieth century.

---

19   R. Albert Mohler Jr., *The Gathering Storm: Secularism, Culture and the Church* (Nashville, TN: Nelson Books, 2020), 24.

In the early twentieth century, the individual came to be defined by
the Social Gospel and progressive movements as the innocent victim
of an unjust capitalist and civil society rather than responsible for his
or her well-being. From the mid-twentieth century, academic social
science reimagined the goal of social justice as required to produce
equality for historically oppressed groups of victims, reflecting
cultural Marxism and multiculturalism.[20]

As Christians, we should mirror God's heart of care for issues such as
racial discrimination, poverty, human trafficking, sexual abuse, and other
injustices or needs. (In preaching the Bible, when I come to a passage that
condemns the sins that contribute to social ills—such as discrimination
or alcohol—I must speak out.) But we should not equate involvement
in these with sharing the gospel or allow involvement here to become a
substitute for directly obeying the Great Commission.

As a Baptist pastor, I believe that soulwinning and gospel preaching
are to be my priorities rather than social justice. Jesus, who healed the
sick and fed the hungry and ministered in other physical ways, said His
chief purpose was saving the lost: "For the Son of man is come to seek
and to save that which was lost" (Luke 19:10).

Again, today's social justice goes back to the New Evangelical
movement of the previous generation. In a book favorable to New
Evangelicalism, the author notes the heavy emphasis of a social agenda
among the movement's leaders:

"The first prominent spokesman calling for a revival of interest
in social issues," argued David Moberg, "was Carl F. H. Henry."
Calling for a "new reformation," Henry's *Uneasy Conscience of*

---

20   William H. Young, "Academic Social Science and Social Justice," *National Association
of Scholars*, August 28, 2015, https://www.nas.org/blogs/dicta/academic_social_
science_and_social_justice.

Modern Fundamentalism spelled out the implications of personal regeneration for social as well as individual problems. Henry minced no words in his indictment of Fundamentalism for its lack of an adequate social agenda.[21]

I am not against Christians speaking out against social injustices. At the beginning of this chapter I mentioned a few Christian leaders who have tackled issues of culturally-accepted injustice head on.

As a local church, however, we have to put a priority somewhere. And the word *priority* means "first." You can only have one true priority. For the church, this priority must remain the Great Commission of Christ.

Yes, God may lead individual Christians to engage in social causes, and He may even give us as spiritual leaders unique opportunities to influence the issues of the day. I think of how William Carey played a significant role in India of bringing the legal end to the barbaric practice of *sati,* the burning alive of an Indian widow when her husband died; or of John Newton's influence to end slavery, especially by encouraging William Wilberforce. But in both cases, the missionary and the pastor mentioned kept their main focus on proclaiming the gospel. Carey is remembered for being the father of modern missions and for his extensive work in Bible translation. Newton is remembered today for his hymn "Amazing Grace" and was primarily known in his lifetime for pastoral work and gospel preaching.

When we pick up the baton of social reform, equating involvement with our primary calling as Christians or as the mission of the local church, all kinds of confusion follows. Issues that are actually clear in Scripture become blurry. For instance, to many Christians engaged in social justice, an issue such as abortion is no longer a straightforward

---

21 Garth M. Rosell, *The Surprising Work of God: Harold John Ockenga, Billy Graham, and the Rebirth of Evangelicalism* (Grand Rapids, MI: Baker Academic, 2008), 165.

issue settled by the biblical truth of the sanctity of life. It has been superseded by "compassion" and the need to care for women in poverty—as if God doesn't compassionately care for these women or their often fatherless children.

Furthermore, because social justice, commonly understood, relates to issues including abortion, welfare, healthcare, the environment, immigration, the definition of marriage, foreign policy, poverty rates, and economics, it's easy to see how a further lack of clarity comes simply by differing views on how these objectives are best served. I can confidently take a biblical position on abortion. But my views on foreign policy are obviously going to be filtered by judgment, best understanding of facts, and personal paradigm. What I have seen happen more than I ever remember in the past is Christians accusing one another of harming the testimony of Christ or being uncompassionate toward those in need simply because they have a different view on an issue that is not strictly biblical. The end result is that while clear moral truths are clouded and less-clear applications of principle are elevated, the gospel itself gets pushed to the side as Christians insist on "living the gospel."

One of the sad casualties of this kind of activism, besides the loss of clarity on truth, is that truly gospel-focused, local church ministry often gets pushed aside in an effort to "love our neighbors" by engaging in secularly-driven social reform.

In addition to the concern about the gospel being *replaced* by social justice, there is a valid concern that the gospel is being *set aside by* social justice. I am concerned that we not undermine the very truths of the gospel by the solutions the social justice movement proposes.

The fact is that the Bible does address the social ills with which social justice claims to deal. But it provides a different remedy than the social justice movement suggests.

For example, Critical Race Theory seeks to right the wrongs of racism but actually *perpetuates* racism. Not only does it call for a kind of ongoing penitence for the sins of one's ancestors, but it basically equates whiteness with privilege and privilege with sin.

Racism was decidedly an issue among first-century Christians due to the social influences of their day and the international impositions of the Roman empire. First-century churches were comprised of people saved out of a variety of backgrounds and prejudices. But when Paul wrote to the church at Colossae, he didn't tell them to become more *woke* and aware of the differences.[22] He told them that in Christ the differences are *abolished:* "Where there is neither Greek nor Jew, circumcision nor uncircumcision, Barbarian, Scythian, bond nor free: but Christ is all, and in all" (Colossians 3:11).

In light of the issues raised by the social justice and woke movements, the next three verses are particularly meaningful to Bible-believing Christians: "Put on therefore, as the elect of God, holy and beloved, bowels of mercies, kindness, humbleness of mind, meekness, longsuffering; Forbearing one another, and forgiving one another, if any man have a quarrel against any: even as Christ forgave you, so also do ye. And above all these things put on charity, which is the bond of perfectness" (Colossians 3:12–14). Do these words describe the defensive, divisive outrage so common, even among Christians, in today's social justice movement?

And what of the doctrine of sin? Proponents of social justice and CRT would have any group which they deem to be privileged to perpetually do penance for the sins of their ancestors. But the Bible specifically teaches

---

22 *Woke* is a term meaning awakened to the systemic oppression of certain minority groups by white Americans. See http://capstonereport.com/2019/10/05/the-wokening-of-the-southern-baptist-convention/33125.

that sin is an individual matter of breaking God's law—not a group social matter absorbed by one's ancestors.

Obviously, there are many nuances and angles from which we can look at the sin of racism. And none of these should allow us to call it anything less than sin. But the gospel answer is directly contrary to the social justice answer. In Christ, we have unity, love, and forgiveness.

THE ANSWER TO SOCIAL JUSTICE

So, what do social justice, CRT, intersectionality, and being woke have to do with contemporary theology for Baptist pastors?

A surface, but legitimate, conclusion is a warning concerning hitching yourself to the social justice bandwagon. It has roots that are absolutely antithetical to the gospel, and it is headed in a direction away from the truth. Throughout this book, I have tried to emphasize that the most significant issues I see are not semantics, but the meanings behind the words. The same is true when it comes to social justice. But for every tenderhearted, compassionate Christian who desires to show the love of Christ to a broken world, it's worth pointing out that the social justice terminology doesn't always mean what you think it means and might cause more confusion than clarity to your message.

Another observational conclusion is that these are difficult issues for the Southern Baptist Convention right now. Several churches have even pulled out of the convention due to related concerns. One church that pulled out explained their reasoning in a letter, as noted in the following article:

> The letter outlined a series of concerns including actions by the Ethics and Religious Liberty Commission (ERLC) of the Southern

Baptist Convention, the progressive political views of ERLC president Russell Moore, questionable teachings presented by Southern Baptist Convention President J. D. Greear, problems with Lifeway's promotion of 'theologically heretical materials,' the promotion of Beth Moore in the SBC and the passage of Resolution 9 praising Critical Race Theory and Intersectionality.[23]

Additionally, the Conservative Baptist Network I noted in chapter 3 was launched, in part, because of concerns related to social justice trends within the SBC.[24] Some have postulated that the pursuit of social justice will be the undoing of the SBC.[25] If you're an independent Baptist pastor, I think it's important to consider the scope of these influences. When I see independent Baptists thinking it's a cool idea to discuss these terms as the focus of a preaching series or attend the conference of the leaders of this movement, I am concerned for their future soundness.

But more importantly than all of this is what is lost in the pursuit of the social justice agenda—namely, the gospel and Christian compassion. Here we circle back to where we began with James 1:27: "Pure religion and undefiled before God and the Father is this, To visit the fatherless and widows in their affliction, and to keep himself unspotted from the world."

Remember George Müller we mentioned at the beginning of this chapter? Interestingly, the years during which he reached street children with the love of Christ and opportunity to receive the gospel (1835–1898)

---

23   "Liberal Politics, Theology Pushes Conservatives out of Southern Baptist Convention," *Capstone Report,* September 27, 2019, http://capstonereport.com/2019/09/27/liberal-politics-theology-pushes-conservatives-out-of-southern-baptist-convention/33087.
24   In the bullets on their home page stating their purpose, they have included a bullet reading, "The Network rejects various unbiblical ideologies currently affecting the Southern Baptist Convention such as Critical Race Theory, intersectionality, and social justice." https://conservativebaptistnetwork.com, accessed March 10, 2020.
25   "Stay and Fight or Leave the Southern Baptist Convention?," *Capstone Report,* October 4, 2019, http://capstonereport.com/2019/10/04/stay-and-fight-or-leave-the-southern-baptist-convention/33121.

covered the same era as Charles Dickens wrote *Oliver Twist* (1837–1839). Dickens' novel certainly had an indirect positive impact on the plight of orphans. But Müller's orphanages had a direct, hands-on involvement. Müller didn't just write about compassion; he practiced it. *That* is the power of the gospel.

That's not to say that journalism, writing, or even political organization cannot impact people in a society for good. They obviously can. But it is to say that direct gospel ministry has a lasting impact that no other form of engagement can have. From Dickens and Müller, one could even draw a parallel between a journalist and a church bus worker. One exposes the needs of underprivileged people in a community. The other goes right into those homes, shows the love of Christ to children who often receive little love, and brings the gospel message—sometimes impacting an entire family for eternity. The role of the journalist is important; the role of the bus worker is essential and eternal.

We as Christians have the answers the world needs, yet will never have on its own. So let's see the problems through a biblical lens and act on the solutions with a gospel focus. We must be the people who love others, do justly, and embrace true unity where the ground is level at the foot of the cross.

CHAPTER TEN

GOSPEL-CENTERED TRENDS

F OR MANY YEARS, MY LIFE VERSE was Romans 1:16: "For I am not ashamed of the gospel of Christ: for it is the power of God unto salvation to every one that believeth; to the Jew first, and also to the Greek."

I love this verse not only because it shows the focus of Paul's ministry was the bold declaration of the gospel, but also because of the emphasis it places on the power of the gospel. Indeed, I have had the privilege of watching the gospel transform lives over and over again. More than 37,000 people have accepted Christ as Savior on our church property over these nearly thirty-four years of ministry.

In 2011, however, after a prolonged season in which I was brought to a greater understanding of my daily need for the power of the gospel, I changed my life verse to Galatians 2:20: "I am crucified with Christ: nevertheless I live; yet not I, but Christ liveth in me: and the life which I now live in the flesh I live by the faith of the Son of God, who loved me, and gave himself for me."

Both verses are about the gospel—one emphasizes the gospel's role in salvation, and the other emphasizes the gospel's role in our daily life and ministry. Our relationship with Christ begins with the gospel and continues through the gospel. The gospel is our foundation, and it is the building. It is the birth of our Christian life, and it is central to every aspect of its growth. From the moment we are saved up through the rest of eternity, we will be discovering the fullness of the gospel and the significance of what it means to be "in Christ."

From this perspective, I appreciate and affirm the gospel-centered trend in ministry today. Placing an emphasis on the power of the gospel for growth in our Christian life and on the gospel itself as the paradigm through which we see our relationship with God can never be a negative.

But there is a difference between using *gospel-centered* as an adjective and using it as a singular paradigm for ministry. When used as a simple description—or even prescription—as the New Testament basis for spiritual growth, it is refreshing. When used as an exclusive paradigm for ministry, it can be limiting, as the author below noted:

> "Gospel-centered" is a popular term and one we may look to as a mark of conformity or orthodoxy, as if using the term is inherently good. However, in some cases it is more of a sales strategy than a theological distinction. Further, not every author means the same thing by it and some authors understand it more fully than others.[1]

In this chapter, I want to explore the biblical centrality of the gospel to our lives as well as concerns related to practices sometimes associated with the gospel-centered trend. My main concerns relate to the kind of emphasis that undermines declarative exposition and application of God's Word.

---

1 Tim Challies, "The Gospel-Centered Everything," *Tim Challies*, March 7, 2013, https://www.challies.com/articles/the-gospel-centered-everything.

CHRIST-CENTERED, GOSPEL-LOVING

The gospel, of course, is the death, burial, and resurrection of Jesus for our sins (1 Corinthians 15:3–4). At first glance, any Baptist would gladly embrace the term *gospel-centered*. We believe in the gospel, actively work to propagate the gospel, and are continually growing in applying the truths of the gospel to our daily lives.

But that's not always how the term *gospel-centered* is used. Often it refers to a style of ministry that wants to be identified almost exclusively with and by the gospel and has a tendency to avoid biblical application that prescribes moral principles to living. What ends up happening, however, is that people start calling *everything* the gospel. To be sure, everything in our Christian life should *relate to* the gospel and be experienced through the *power of* the gospel. But *everything* is not the gospel. This is a weakness that even proponents of this movement have pointed out, as seen in the quote below:

> In all of this, we do need to be careful not to see the term *gospel* as a sort of junk drawer that holds any and every piece of our theology. Although the gospel does impact everything, everything is not the gospel. If everything about Jesus and the Bible becomes "the gospel" to us, then we end up being gospel-confused rather than gospel-centered.[2]

Jerry Vines said something similar to me in a conversation related to this topic: "Sometimes if we're not careful, we can make a word cover everything so it ends up covering nothing. And I think *gospel* is one of those words that has been misused. If everything is the gospel, then nothing is the gospel." He further cautioned, "We must be careful

---

2   Matt Chandler, Eric Geiger, Josh Patterson, *Creature of the Word* (Nashville, TN: B&H Books, 2012), 7.

that the word *gospel* is not a code word for a man-centered theology or methodology, but that it is a clear word for a *God*-centered theology and methodology."

I prefer the term *Christ-centered* as a ministry adjective over *gospel-centered*. This is partly because it has less identification with a movement that is largely led by people whose doctrine and ministry philosophy I don't share, but primarily I prefer *Christ-centered* because it emphasizes our personal relationship with Christ. The Bible is about Jesus. The gospel is through Jesus. And my motivation to serve *is* Jesus!

I also prefer the term *Christ-centered* from a theological perspective. The opposite of man-centered theology is not *gospel*-centered, but *God*-centered. Indeed, the center of good theology is the God who acts, not the actions of God. What God has done for me is secondary to who God is to me. Thus, while the gospel is the way God has delivered His grace to me, I want my focus to be on and my motivation to come from Christ Himself.

Another reason I don't readily use the term *gospel-centered* is because of the division that has grown up around it. It's sad to me that there has come a division over the very word *gospel*. In part, this has happened because, as we said a moment ago, the term means so many different things to different people, and semantics in general can become confusing. Over the years, people have used terms (often as accusations) like easy believism, hard believism, performancism, non-performancism, grace based, hyper grace, gospel everything, gospel nothing . . . . Sometimes the terms just become more noise among people who already share common doctrine. And sometimes people use nuances of semantics to create division.

It is ironic that some of those who most loudly hold to a gospel-centered label can be the most un-Christlike in despising those who they don't believe are gospel centered enough. As I was finishing writing this chapter, I received a letter from a young preacher sharing frustration regarding this spirit of division. He had previously looked up to those who placed an emphasis on the gospel as our center, but in interpersonal interactions he had experienced an ungracious spirit from those he had admired. He wrote, "You know that I've wrestled with the whole gospel-centered conversation. This week, I got a crystal clear picture of the fruit of the doubt and division it is causing . . . the spirit with which it is being promoted, and I decidedly affirmed that I am NOT interested in being any part of that."

Remember that biblical gospel-centeredness is about saturating your heart in the good news of Jesus' death, burial, and resurrection for our sins. It is about letting the gospel remake your mind about yourself and your life. It's not about discerning if others who believe the same doctrines as you apply them thoroughly enough. J. D. Greear, with whom I have disagreed earlier in this book, made a good point in this area in his book *Gospel:* "The point of gospel-centeredness, however, is not the shrewd ability to critique others. The point of gospel-centeredness is to adore God . . . ."[3]

HOW THE GOSPEL SHOULD SHAPE MINISTRY

There are commendable traits of the gospel-centered movement. Although there are many distinctions individual leaders might make, generally speaking, the following are strong earmarks of those who identify as gospel-centered:

---

3   J. D. Greear, *Gospel: Recovering the Power that Made Christianity Revolutionary* (Nashville, TN: B&H Publishing Group, 2013), 253.

- Seek to be properly motivated by the power of Christ
- Seek to develop truth from a Scripture text itself, rather than going directly to application in preaching
- Seek to develop gospel truth from every Scripture passage, especially the Old Testament
- Seek to be less authoritarian as the authority is all of Christ
- Seek to flee moralism and rules-based holiness
- Seek less program emphasis and more Holy Spirit-prompted ministry

All of these are good and needful goals. But if they become the sole paradigm through which one sees or a measuring stick to evaluate other people and ministries, they can become detrimental.

Through the remainder of this chapter, I'd like to develop six truths relative to gospel-centered ministry, pointing out areas where I believe the gospel-centered movement as a whole sometimes distorts these truths. Because the term itself actually is a tremendous way to encapsulate the message of the New Testament, however, I am organizing this chapter around practical admonitions of how the gospel should define our ministry.

We must lead and motivate by the love of Christ.

It is obvious when you study the life of the apostle Paul that he never got over the fact that the Son of God had personally died for his sin. The love of Christ motivated Paul like perhaps no other motivation in his life: "For the love of Christ constraineth us; because we thus judge, that if one died for all, then were all dead: And that he died for all, that they which live should not henceforth live unto themselves, but unto him which died for them, and rose again" (2 Corinthians 5:14–15).

This is one of the areas where the gospel-centered movement gets it right. If we try to persuade people to serve the Lord or to grow spiritually with guilt, fear, our acceptance, or other lesser motivations, we miss the most powerful motivation embedded into our new life in Christ— the love of Christ in the gospel. Carnal motivations won't last over the decades. In fact, if the dominant theme of our ministries is controlling others rather than serving others, the likeliness of developing strong spiritual leaders will diminish.

We ourselves must be motivated by the gospel—constrained by the love of Christ—and we must point others to His love as well.

We must avoid the trap of performance-based acceptance.

One of the fears of the gospel-centered movement should be something all of us fear as well: creating a sense of performance-based acceptance in others. When a leader focuses on creating behavioral lists, he can unintentionally establish an environment that says, "You are accepted when you meet these criteria." Regardless of how clearly we articulate gospel-based truth, if we withhold acceptance from new Christians until they outwardly conform, or if we give acceptance based on their program involvement, we undermine the message we are trying to preach. It is vital that we understand and preach the truth from Ephesians 1:6 that we are "accepted in the beloved." We don't serve the Lord to prove anything. We serve because Jesus paid everything. It is the love of Christ that constrains us to serve (2 Corinthians 5:14).

Over programming itself is a true concern in many churches. A heavy program—where virtually every evening of the week, year round, holds an all-church event—can indeed be burdensome. Pastors must use care in planning.

Some years ago, I remember being in a Sunday evening service where the pastor asked all those who planned to go soulwinning on Thursday night to stand. The pastor had created an unintentional moral dilemma for a friend of mine who had a family commitment on Thursday. The pastor thought that by engaging public declarations of good intentions, he was helping people to commit to a good and gospel-centered activity. But the way it felt to my friend was more like a guilt trap. He couldn't win either way.

Acceptance through performance only aggravates the root problem of pride. Acceptance through unconditional love is the optimum environment for true growth.

We should not use our liberty as an occasion to the flesh.

While we stand against performance-based teachings and ministry cultures, we also stand against the modern concepts of grace that tend to license. In an effort to avoid *moralism*—the belief that morals earn us favor or grace with God—some avoid preaching or teaching on the pursuit of holy living at all.

I believe this is an overcorrection to a true problem. Sometimes a young leader, either through direct teaching or the natural bent of his human heart, lives for a period of time under the assumption that after his salvation holy living makes him more able to receive God's grace, rather than understanding that God's freely given grace makes him able to practice holy living (Titus 2:11–12). At some point, through the Spirit's power and the Word of God, he realizes that the gospel reaches beyond his salvation to his sanctification, that he is fully accepted in Christ, and that grace is as much a gift today as it was the day he was saved. That is a good day.

Because this breakthrough is so profound, however, the tendency is to see it as a different plane of spiritual truth, rather than personal growth in grace through the work of the Holy Spirit. Now, rather than giving thanks for this new understanding and seeing his current ministry environment in a new gospel-reflecting light, he sees previous experiences and teaching in opposition to gospel grace. This may or may not be true. But with some who are excited at their new identity, there is often a lack of gospel grace shown toward other believers.

Basking in his newly-found freedom in Christ to enjoy God's love, he distances himself from any teaching or beliefs regarding specific, outwardly-visible growth in Christ. It's as if there becomes an inability to distinguish between enjoying the position we have in Christ from living it out through the power of the gospel. He may even become critical of those who don't preach these truths in every message. This experience is more than a "grace awakening." It also can be an "anger awakening" toward his early Christian life.

Grace, rightly lived, produces godliness—not license or defensiveness. Galatians 5:13 warns, "For, brethren, ye have been called unto liberty; only use not liberty for an occasion to the flesh, but by love serve one another." When to some, being gospel-centered means *less* church so they can "live" the gospel, I'm concerned. In the book *Grace Gone Wild*, Robert Jeffress wrote: "I believe that a distortion of grace is largely responsible for the apathy many Christians demonstrate toward their local congregations. Whenever the importance of membership, the necessity of attendance, the expectations for giving, the responsibility of service, and the need for purity within a local congregation are upheld, the proponents of bad grace yell, 'Legalism!'"[4]

---

4   Robert Jeffress, *Grace Gone Wild!: Getting a Grip on God's Amazing Gift* (Colorado Springs, CO: WaterBrook Press, 2005), 145.

I wrote about this concern years ago in *Grace for Godly Living*: "Teachings about grace which de-emphasize righteous living have snared many Christians. . . . These teachings often view grace as a form of license to live according to one's own will. . . . This often becomes a stumbling block and a hindrance to their walk of progressive sanctification."[5]

Moralism and legalism do kill. A focus on grace as a superior understanding of the gospel, however, can bring a pride that kills as well. It becomes an inverted legalism that leads to a sense of condescension toward others.

John Newton gave an insightful comment on the ridiculousness of taking pride in our understanding of grace. Although I'm not a Calvinist and disagree with aspects of his understanding of grace, his larger point is relevant to this discussion:

> And I am afraid there are Calvinists, who, while they account it a proof of their humility that they are willing in words to debase the creature, and to give all the glory of salvation to the Lord, yet know not what manner of spirit they are of. *Whatever it be that makes us trust in ourselves that we are comparatively wise or good, so as to treat those with contempt who do not subscribe to our doctrines, or follow our party, is a proof and fruit of a self-righteous spirit. Self-righteousness can feed upon doctrines, as well as upon works; and a man may have the heart of a Pharisee, while his head is stored with orthodox notions of the unworthiness of the creature and the riches of free grace* (emphasis added).[6]

---

5   Paul Chappell, *Grace for Godly Living: Allowing God's Grace to Produce a Godly Life* (Lancaster, CA: Striving Together Publications, 2009), 7.

6   John Newton, *The Works of the Rev. John Newton . . . : To which are Prefixed Memoirs of His Life* (London: T. Nelson and Sons, 1853), 80.

The answer is not less gospel or more grace. The answer is a wider view that takes in the entire Word of God. It is true that we are "accepted in the beloved" (Ephesians 1:6) and that there is nothing we can do that will make God love us any more than He already does (Romans 8:35–39). *And* it is true that it is possible to resist the Holy Spirit's work in our life. This is why 1 Thessalonians 5:19 commands, "Quench not the Spirit."

If we only preach and teach on God's acceptance in Christ through the gospel and fail to admonish people to use the freedom the gospel gives them to obey (see Romans 6), they miss out on the daily experience of gospel freedom. It's like telling Americans they have freedom of speech and then allowing them to throw chairs through coffee shop windows in violent protests. The right to freedom of speech is useless without a valid interpretation of freedom. Similarly, when it comes to freedom in Christ, we must uplift the truth of our acceptance in the beloved *and* our responsibility to work out our own salvation with fear and trembling (Philippians 2:12).

We must teach the whole counsel of God.

Some advocates of gospel-centeredness avoid preaching applications that put responsibility on the hearer. Their reasoning is that all of Scripture is tied to the gospel and their job in each sermon is to bring the text back to the gospel. The result is a church family missing out on discovering how the gospel calls us to and empowers us in real life choices. In an effort to bring spiritual grace, it brings spiritual weakness.

Teaching the commands of the New Testament does not violate New Testament gospel-centeredness. You cannot separate the precepts of Jesus from the person of Jesus.

One author, criticizing preachers who he doesn't believe are gospel-centered, wrote the following:

> If a preacher exposits, verse-by-verse, books of the Bible focusing on
> moral, ethical, behavioral and attitudinal change, without mediating
> the meaning and application of the text through Jesus, he teaches a
> dangerous lesson. . . . Such moralistic preaching communicates that
> after believers walk through the gospel door, their focus should be
> keeping God's rules, learning timeless principles, and noting which
> biblical characters to emulate and which to spurn.[7]

I understand and agree with his larger point. But his nuances in judgment bring some challenges. For instance, the phrase "without mediating the meaning and application of the text through Jesus" is hard to objectively quantify. We need to be careful that we don't superimpose our expectations for gospel-centered verbiage in exposition or application on others. Furthermore, I believe to be rightly dividing truth, it is needful for me to preach through books of the Bible, including the pastoral epistles, verse by verse.

The gospel-only hermeneutical emphasis seems to be a reaction against preaching that may have been solely topical in nature, but the ditch on the other side of the road is a deemphasis on the line-by-line exposition of God's Word. Moving away from lists of conformance is commendable, but we must not neglect scriptural admonition in our demand that every message meet our personal paradigm of interpretation. If a preacher is rightly dividing the Word in a text that gives practical admonitions (such as 1 Thessalonians 5:19–22), he may be accused of being a moralistic list reader or even a legalist for not preaching the hermeneutical path defined by recent books. I've heard self-identifying gospel-centered leaders speak dismissively of sermons from godly, faithful men because they didn't

---

7   David E. Prince, "What God Has Joined Together: Indicatives and Imperatives," *The Ethics & Religious Liberty Commission*, March 10, 2014 https://erlc.com/resource-library/articles/what-god-has-joined-together-indicatives-and-imperatives.

bring an Old Testament passage back to Christ. Would it be good if they had? Of course. But can I respect them for their faithfulness to the texts and the truths they did draw from the passage? Absolutely.

We know that the New Testament provides both indicatives and imperatives. The indicatives are statements of fact: "And you hath he quickened, who were dead in trespasses and sins" (Ephesians 2:1). The imperatives are commands or instruction: "And be ye kind one to another, tenderhearted, forgiving one another, even as God for Christ's sake hath forgiven you" (Ephesians 4:32).

A moralistic message from Ephesians 4:32 would basically say, "It's right to forgive. God wants you to forgive. So be more forgiving." A gospel-centered message from this passage would include emphasis on the reality that we are forgiven in Christ and that His forgiveness gives us both the motivation and ability to forgive others. (This one is pretty easy since Christ's forgiveness for us is right in the verse.)

But here is where we need to be careful. At what point in the message do the gospel imperatives regarding God's forgiveness through Christ need to be included? And how often? Does it need to be the entire first point? Or can it be included throughout the text? Are there ever times when it might be okay if a preacher is aware of having recently preached indicative-rich messages and leans toward an imperative-rich message? What if a pastor is preaching through a Pauline epistle and follows the pattern in which Paul wrote, where the first half of messages on the epistle lean more toward indicatives and the second half more toward imperatives? Is he still gospel-centered?

Do you see where using *gospel-centered* as an interpretive philosophy of ministry can become muddy? The reality is that the better we understand the gospel and its connection to every aspect of God's Word, the more it will permeate our thoughts, living, and preaching. This growth is a lifelong process.

Gospel-centered preachers can and must exhort their congregations from God's Word. They must preach "all the counsel of God" (Acts 20:27). They must not preach only the gospel indicatives (as important and foundational as those are), but they must teach the commands of God.

We must take care that we don't use the *idea* of the gospel to neglect the *application* of the gospel. It is not necessarily moralistic to preach the morals of God's Word, any more than it was for Paul to instruct, reprimand, and exhort the Corinthian church in relation to specific areas of moral sin. Both the grace of God and the commands of the New Testament have a role in teaching us and forming us spiritually. Any emphasis on gospel-centered ministry that diminishes the role of biblical commands can lead toward antinomian ism.

So yes, our motivation must not be guilt or fear, but the love of Christ. Yet being gospel-*centered* should not mean being gospel *only*. We need admonitions and instructions, but we need to bring it all back to the cross.

Even the Calvinist teacher John Piper points out that the gospel-centered focus can minimize sanctification. He has two main concerns. First, he notes that gospel-only preaching is "deficient in showing the whole purpose of the cross." After all, Jesus in "his own self bare our sins in his own body on the tree, that we, *being dead to sins, should live unto righteousness: by whose stripes ye were healed*" (1 Peter 2:24). So if we only discuss Christ's bearing our sins but neglect His making us dead to self and enabled to live unto righteousness, we miss out on a huge part of why Christ saved us.

Piper's other concern with some gospel-centered preachers is that "they are reticent to draw attention to the law of Christ, but instead of drawing attention to all these commandments, they say ... 'You can't keep the law. Christ did it for you. Trust the imputation of Christ's forgiveness. End of sermon. Celebrate.'"[8] As Piper points out, this is based on a shallow understanding of the law and Christ's imputed righteousness.

James 1:25 specifically admonishes us to look into the Bible as "the perfect law of liberty" and to not be "a forgetful hearer, but a doer of the work." The fact is that we *can* live a biblical life in the power of the Holy Spirit, and when we do, it brings liberty in our hearts. Justification and sanctification are both aspects of salvation. Justification is what God does *for* a sinner, while sanctification is what God does *in* a sinner. In fact, God directly commands us to obey as He empowers, which is the ongoing process of sanctification.

We need both the indicatives *and* the imperatives. We need the imputed righteousness of Christ *and* the power to obey His commands.

Perhaps my favorite illustration of the indicatives and imperatives of Scripture is an analogy I heard some time ago that likened the commands of Scripture to train tracks and the gospel to the engine. Just as the tracks do nothing to power the train, so the commands of God's Word are not where we get our power for the Christian life. We need the power of the gospel that breaks sin's hold and gives us the ability to obey God from new, regenerated hearts. That is our engine. And it is an engine that empowers us along the tracks of God's commands.

We must preach against sin.

Some preachers, in an effort to highlight the gospel without seeming judgmental to unsaved people, avoid preaching against specific sins, but

---

8   John Piper, "Two Dangers in 'Gospel-Centered' Preaching," YouTube video, 6:48, posted by "Desiring God," February 15, 2019, https://youtu.be/5PcmDFhQx6o.

feel they can simply point out the general reality that we are all sinners. This goes back to our discussion on contexutalization, but it applies here as well. Preaching against sin does not violate gospel-centeredness. In fact, without the preaching of sin, there is no need for the gospel (Romans 7:7).

Jesus preached the gospel, but he also preached against the sins of the day. Jonah, who preached a message of repentance that led to God's outpouring of grace, was instructed to cry against the great wickedness of Nineveh: "Now the word of the LORD came unto Jonah the son of Amittai, saying, Arise, go to Nineveh, that great city, and cry against it; for their wickedness is come up before me" (Jonah 1:1–2).

This is not a popular message for the modern church, but part of the responsibility of preaching is reminding unsaved people of the God who will judge: "And he commanded us to preach unto the people, and to testify that it is he which was ordained of God to be the Judge of quick and dead" (Acts 10:42).

We must avoid the Calvinism in books that are written about the gospel-centered movement.

Many authors who identify as gospel-centered are proponents of a limited atonement. This goes against the very nature of the gospel itself—God's free offer of salvation through Christ.

The Bible genuinely gives a universal offer of salvation to all—not to only a select few. As Jesus told Nicodemus in John 3:16, "For God so loved the world, that he gave his only begotten Son, that *whosoever* believeth in him should not perish, but have everlasting life." The word *whosoever* in this verse is translated from the Greek word *pas,* which is used 1,228 times in the New Testament. Gehard Kittel, in the *Theological Dictionary of the New Testament,* says it means "a totality and an inclusion of all individual parts."[9] Another way to say it is that it means, well, *whosoever.* God has given man a free will, and man of his own belief or volition may turn to Christ. As one author said, "The word is a welcome mat inviting the world to God. . . . The idea is non-restrictive. The idea is anyone . . . anywhere . . . anytime."[10]

First John 2:2 specifically tells us that Christ died "for the sins of the whole world." First Timothy 2:4 tells us that God "will have all men to be saved, and to come unto the knowledge of the truth." And 2 Peter 3:9 says, "The Lord is . . . not willing that any should perish, but that all should come to repentance."

As desperately as we need to preach the gospel to ourselves every day of our lives and as important as it is to teach and preach through a biblical framework that functionally applies the gospel to our daily living, we should be careful that our fundamental input of what it means to be gospel-centered comes from God's Word and not from those who limit the invitation of the gospel.

Furthermore, we should be careful that being "gospel-centered" includes actually sharing the gospel with the lost. When our gospel hermeneutic is more about license than soulwinning, it can become self- serving. Our goal in the Christian life isn't simply to understand how to better apply the gospel in our own lives and how to most clearly articulate gospel truths to other Christians. In a blog post critiquing a section of the gospel-centered movement, Jeff Amsbaugh highlighted the tendency of some leaders to shy away from direct evangelism:

> Keller, as many others . . . has shunned both "evangelical" and
> "fundamentalist" labels because of their political connotations. The

9   B. Reicke, "pas," in *The Theological Dictionary of the New Testament* (ed. G. Kittel and G. Friedrich; Grand Rapids, MI: Eerdmans, 1969), 5:887.

10   David Allen and Steve W. Lemke, eds., *Whosoever Will A Biblical-Theological Critique of Five-Point Calvinism* (Nashville, TN: B&H Publishing Group, 2010), 24.

thought is that the abrasiveness of fundamentalism is actually a deterrent to evangelism, and a softer, milder approach is in order. As mentioned earlier, I too have concerns about being harsh and anti-intellectual in our methods. But I'm concerned that the Gospel-centered movement has taken this much further *so that leaders are ashamed of truth and unwilling to take an uncompromising stand or to confront people with their need for salvation* (emphasis added).[11]

Our calling and our goal is the Great Commission of Christ. Being gospel-centered needs to, at a very foundational level, include gospel passion to share the offer of salvation with whosoever will hear and believe. The gospel is for all, and we must tell it!

WE PREACH CHRIST

Ultimately, when it comes to any self-identifying interpretations of ministry, we must remember that our highest purpose in ministry is to "preach Christ crucified" (1 Corinthians 1:23).

Yes, we want to contextualize our message so all who hear it understand. Yes, we want to emphasize our mission so that it is embedded into every part of our lives. Yes, we want to be gospel-centric in every aspect of our walk with God and ministry focus. But if our identity is defined by our styles of ministry, we run the risk of forgetting Jesus Himself.

My identity is that I am washed by the blood of Christ, sealed by the Holy Spirit, and called as a minister of the gospel. My identity is *Christ*.

May we not get so caught up in identifying labels—whether they be "old paths," "relevant," "gospel-centered," or "grace-driven"—that we miss

---

11 Jeff Amsbaugh, "Observations about the Gospel-Centered Interpretation of Ministry," *Ministry 127*, May 21, 2018, https://ministry127.com/pastoral-leadership/observations-about-the-gospel-centered-interpretation-of-ministry.

the joy of Galatians 2:20: "I am crucified with Christ: nevertheless I live; yet not I, but Christ liveth in me: and the life which I now live in the flesh I live by the faith of the Son of God, who loved me, and gave himself for me."

I'm for labels because they are helpful ways to identify what we believe and practice. But I never want to get so wrapped up in a movement or other people's positions that I preach the gospel more for my peers than I do for the lost. "For we preach not ourselves, but Christ Jesus the Lord . . ." (2 Corinthians 4:5).

CHAPTER ELEVEN

RADICAL GRACE TRENDS

Early in John Bunyan's allegorical book *The Pilgrim's Progress,* the main character, Christian, is turned out of the way leading to the cross by Mr. Worldly Wiseman who tells him there is an easier way:

> Why, in yonder Village (the village is named *Morality)* there dwells a gentleman whose name is *Legality,* a very judicious man (and a man of a very good name) that has skill to help men off with such Burdens as is thine, from their shoulders; yea, to my knowledge, he hath done a great deal of good this way: Ay, and besides, he hath skill to cure those that are somewhat crazed in their wits with their Burdens. To him, as I said, thou may'st go, and be helped presently. His house is not quite a mile from this place; and if he should not be at home himself, he hath a pretty young man to his Son, whose name is *Civility,* that can do it (to speak on) as well as the old Gentleman himself: There, I say, thou may'st be eased of thy Burden . . . .

Christian follows these instructions and finds himself unable to meet the demands of Morality:

> So *Christian* turned out of his way to go to Mr. *Legality's* house for help: But behold, when he was got now hard by the Hill, it seemed so high, and also that side of it that was next the Wayside, did hang so much over, that *Christian* was afraid to venture farther, lest the Hill should fall on his head; wherefore there he stood still, and he wot not what to do. Also his Burden now seemed heavier to him than while he was in his Way. There came also flashes of fire out of the Hill, that made *Christian* afraid that he should be burned: Here, therefore, he sweat and did quake for Fear.[1]

In Bunyan's insightful writing, human pride is turned on its head as Christian finally realizes he cannot meet the demands of the law. The burden of our sin, especially such a burden when we are under the conviction of the Holy Spirit as Christian was, grows no lighter by rule-keeping.

Enter *grace*.

God's grace was so lavishly poured out by Jesus on the cross that there are no words to properly describe it. Even John Newton's adjective *amazing* falls short.

Grace is radical. It is undeserved. It is overwhelming. It is, well, *amazing*.

Furthermore, grace doesn't need to be balanced—as if you could have too much of it and must only receive it in moderation or in proportion to your effort. Actually, grace *abounds*. That's what Romans 5:20 tells us: "Moreover the law entered, that the offence might abound. But where sin abounded, grace did much more abound."

Grace doesn't need to be balanced or held back. But it does need to be properly understood. And that understanding was Paul's care as he finished Romans 5 and transitioned into Romans 6. He wasn't afraid that

---

1   John Bunyan, *The Pilgrim's Progress* (Uhrichsville, OH: Barbour, 1988), 24–25.

people would receive too much grace; he was afraid that they would take God's grace for granted: "What shall we say then? Shall we continue in sin, that grace may abound? God forbid. How shall we, that are dead to sin, live any longer therein?" (Romans 6:1–2).

The rest of Romans 6 explains that grace is not our license to sin; rather, grace is our freedom out of the bondage of sin. This is not only true in the sense of the penalty of sin, but it is also true in the daily routines of our lives. Properly understood and applied, God's grace liberates us from habitual, besetting sins and gives us the ability to live as servants of God.

Of course, this doesn't mean we attain sinless perfection. Romans 7 makes that clear. We aren't fighting this war against sin in a vacuum, for we still struggle against the flesh. In the midst of our struggle, grace gives us the power to fight victoriously. And Romans 8 assures us that the Holy Spirit helps us in the battle and doesn't withhold His love or acceptance based on our daily progress.

There are some, however, who teach a skewed message of grace that, while claiming to give a "fuller" understanding, actually weaken and cheapen grace. Although usually labeling another position as *hyper* is a pejorative term used by those who disagree with that position (e.g. hyper Calvinist or hyper separatist), in this case, it is actually claimed by those who promote the position. One of these men, Paul Ellis, wrote a book titled *Hyper Grace Gospel.* Because Ellis, Joseph Prince, Steve McVey, and Andrew Farley are some of the key proponents of this position, I'll quote from their books in this chapter as we look at these doctrinal trends and answer them with the truths of Scripture.

As mentioned in our previous chapter, some of those who express radical grace say, in effect, "You can't live the Christian life, but Jesus lived it for you. Celebrate grace." There is truth to those statements. You and I can*not* live the Christian life in our strength. And Jesus *did* live it for us. The imputed righteousness of God is one of the most precious doctrines in Scripture. "For he hath made him to be sin for us, who knew no sin; that we might be made the righteousness of God in him" (2 Corinthians 5:21).

But that is only *part* of God's grace. And the part that continues only gets better. Not only has Christ imputed His righteousness to us, but He has given us the Holy Spirit who enables us to live a Christlike life.

> Now the Lord is that Spirit: and where the Spirit of the Lord is, there is liberty. But we all, with open face beholding as in a glass the glory of the Lord, are changed into the same image from glory to glory, even as by the Spirit of the Lord.
> —2 CORINTHIANS 3:17–18

> This I say then, Walk in the Spirit, and ye shall not fulfil the lust of the flesh. . . . If we live in the Spirit, let us also walk in the Spirit.
> —GALATIANS 5:16, 25

A better statement, then, would be, "You can't live the Christian life, but Jesus lived it for you, and now, the Holy Spirit desires to live it *through* you. Celebrate grace!"

Any teaching of grace that minimizes our responsibility to live a Christlike life through the Holy Spirit's enabling misunderstands grace. Furthermore, any teaching of grace that dismisses the commands of God as mere "law" and suggests every biblical instruction has been abolished by Christ undervalues the power available to us by the Spirit of God. Grace is not license to sin; it is empowerment to Christlikeness.

Even Timothy Keller, an author I have disagreed with previously in this book, warns of the "error of antinomianism, an attitude that is afraid to ever say, 'You ought,' and refrains from insisting that God's law must be obeyed."[2]

---

2   Timothy Keller, *Center Church: Doing Balanced, Gospel-Centered Ministry in Your City* (Grand Rapids, MI: Zondervan, 2012), 48.

In the next few pages, I'd like to ask and answer two questions related to specific areas in which the hyper-grace movement misappropriates and misunderstands grace—the law and confession—and then follow with some general observations as to why this matters so much for gospel ministry.

SO WHAT ABOUT THE LAW?

There are those in the radical grace movement who, ignoring the various ways "the law" is used throughout the Bible, interpret *any* expectation of obedience or command of Scripture as "law." For instance, Andrew Farley writes, "Rules are the same as law. Rules assume we are dirty and distant from God."[3]

While we are no longer "under the law" in the sense that we are not judged by it because Christ has perfectly fulfilled it for us (see the entire book of Galatians), we are still to obey Christ's commands out of obedience to Him (John 14:15). There is, in fact, a distinction throughout the New Testament in how the word *law* is used. Where Paul speaks of not being "under the law" (such as in Galatians 3:2, 4:21) he is referring to the Law of Moses. Elsewhere, however, we learn that as New Testament believers, we are under the "law of Christ" (Galatians 6:2) and the "perfect law of liberty" (James 1:25).

In his helpful dissertation on this subject, Daniel Stevens observed, "To the radical grace teacher any 'law' is contrary to the message of grace. At times, they are dealing with law in general in the life of a Christian and

---

3   Andrew Farley, *Heaven Is Now: Awakening Your Five Spiritual Senses to the Wonders of Grace* (Grand Rapids, MI: Baker Books, 2012), 33.

under this umbrella they incorporate the Old Testament Law. To these men law equals rules, which would be the enemy of grace."[4]

Paul Ellis, a proponent of hyper-grace philosophy writes:

> A mixed-grace gospel mixes law with grace and reaps the benefits of neither. It promotes the law as a guide for living and treats grace as little more than a lubricant for greasing the cogs of self-effort. Those who buy into this message reveal their disregard for both law, since they cannot keep it yet pretend to, and grace, since they would rather trust in their own efforts than in Christ's magnificent work. Such a person is lukewarm. They have not yielded to either the cold and unbending demands of the law or the white-hot love and grace of their Father.[5]

Once you look past the out-of-context use of Scripture phrases in the quote above, you see that by pitting grace against obedience, the author is actually disregarding grace. No, we can't "keep the law." But we can, by the grace of God expressed through the power of the Holy Spirit, obey our Heavenly Father.

It seems that out of a reaction to teaching that we obey to gain favor with God (which is not true), these teachers have gone to the opposite extreme to say we don't need to obey at all. The truth is that we can only obey God through the power of the Holy Spirit, and we do so out of love for Him.

We cannot neglect the clear commands of Scripture in favor of grace, as if there were somehow disunity in God's Word. The same God who freely offers us His grace tells us that this grace is not for license, but that it teaches us to deny fleshly living: "For the grace of God that bringeth

---

4   Daniel Stevens, "An Analysis and Evaluation of the Radical Grace Preachers Joseph Prince, Steve Mcvey, Paul Ellis, and Andrew Farley," PhD diss., Piedmont International University, Winston-Salem, 2017, Piedmont International University Library.

5   Paul Ellis, *The Hyper-Grace Gospel* (Birkenhead, New Zealand: KingsPress, 2014), 36.

salvation hath appeared to all men, Teaching us that, denying ungodliness and worldly lusts, we should live soberly, righteously, and godly, *in this present world*" (Titus 2:11–12).

The phrase "in this present world" leads us to what I believe is a key misunderstanding in the radical grace movement—the distinction between our position in Christ and our practice as children of God. Notably, this impacts the area of confession of sin.

WHAT ABOUT CONFESSION?

One of the basic truths seen throughout the New Testament is the immediate and progressive works of salvation.

Immediately, when we trust Christ as our Savior, we are saved from the penalty of sin (Romans 6:23) and receive the Holy Spirit (Ephesians 1:13). We receive the righteousness of God imputed to our account and are, in the eternal presence of God, seated with Christ in heavenly places (Ephesians 1:3).

But we still live on a sin-cursed earth, and we still battle the world, the flesh, and the devil. So while our position in Christ is settled—there is absolutely nothing we do or don't do that will change our sonship with the Father—we live in an arena in which we are called to daily appropriate the resources God has given us to live like the sons of God that we are.

God's ultimate purpose for us is to be conformed to the image of Christ (Romans 8:29), but this is the process of a lifetime. And in that process, victory over sin comes as we practice living out our position in Christ.

But here is where the radical grace teachers get it wrong: they fail to distinguish between position and practice. In attempting to magnify the grace of God, they minimize the obedience of the believer. In attempting to emphasize the acceptance of Christ, they deny the need for a Christian's repentance of sin.

Jerry Vines once said about this issue of repentance as a Christian, "I would assume that I have repented far more after I got saved than before I got saved. As I have grown and hopefully matured in grace, I've seen my sin in a different light more and more, and it's caused *more* repentance on my part."

Most preachers I know and most commentaries teach that 1 John 1:9 is written to Christians and is an encouragement and admonition to stay in close and open fellowship with God: "If we confess our sins, he is faithful and just to forgive us our sins, and to cleanse us from all unrighteousness." But radical grace teachers disagree. They believe it was written to the unbeliever, and they hold this view for two reasons: First, they believe that since we cannot be forgiven for that which Christ already forgave us, the verse (with its promise of forgiveness for confession) must be written to the unsaved. Second, they claim that you can't be "out of fellowship" with the Father when He lives in you. Let's answer both of these arguments.

Does a Christian need forgiveness?

First John 1:9 was absolutely written to Christians. In fact, the entire epistle was written to Christians. From chapter 1 which says it was written that their "joy may be full" (verse 4) to chapter 5 which says the purpose of the epistle was that they would be assured of their salvation (verse 13), there are references in every chapter to Christians. Twice (2:1 and 3:18), John addresses his readers as "my little children."

So if it was written to Christians and if God has already forgiven our sins, what is the confession and forgiveness in this verse talking about? The answer is simple, and it lies in the difference between what we could call *forensic* forgiveness and *familial* forgiveness. One author, answering similar concerns as we are looking at, explained it this way:

> This viewpoint fails to distinguish between *forensic* forgiveness, that we receive at conversion, and *family* forgiveness, that we need after conversion. . . . The fact that God has removed the penalty for our sins at conversion (1 Corinthians 6:11; Ephesians 1:7, 4:32; Colossians 2:13) does not remove the necessity of confessing our sins frequently. Again, the issue is not *acceptance by* God, but *fellowship with* God. *Conversion* (forensic, positional) *forgiveness* makes us acceptable as members of God's family. *Continual* (family, practical) *forgiveness* enables us to experience intimate fellowship as sons within God's family.[6]

In his book *Systematic Theology*, Wayne Grudem explains:

> It is in the context of this relationship with God as our heavenly Father that we are to understand the prayer that Jesus told his disciples to pray daily, *"Our Father who art in heaven . . . forgive us our sins,* as we have also forgiven those who sin against us" (Matthew 6:9–12, author's translation). This daily prayer for forgiveness of sins is not a prayer that God would give us justification again and again throughout our lives, for justification is a one-time event that occurs immediately after we trust in Christ with saving faith. Rather, the prayer for forgiveness of sins each day is a prayer that God's fatherly relationship with us, which has been disrupted by sin that displeased him, be restored, and that he relate to us once again as a Father who delights in his children whom he loves. The prayer, "Forgive us our sins," therefore, is one in which we are relating not to God as eternal judge of the universe, but to God as a Father. It is a prayer in which

---

6   Thomas L. Constable, "Notes on 1 John 2017 edition," *Sonic Light*, accessed August 21, 2017, www.soniclight.com/constable/notes.pdf.1john.pdf.

we wish to restore the open fellowship with our Father that has been broken because of sin.[7]

When we trusted Christ as our Savior, we were justified—declared righteous before God (Romans 5:1). Through the substitutionary sacrifice of Christ, we have the imputed righteousness of God.

But this does not mean that sin has no effect on our relationship with God. Although sin will never change our legal standing with God or the heart of the Father toward us as His children, He still calls us to confess it to Him and receive His forgiveness.

It is much the same as the relationship between me and my four children. There is nothing in this world they can do that would cause me to disown them or push them away. But there are things they could do that would strain our relationship, and if they refused to acknowledge these, it would be impossible to have true familial fellowship and harmony.

This leads us to the second claim of the hyper-grace teacher: that you cannot be out of fellowship with God since He lives in you.

Can a Christian lose fellowship with God?

So what does the Bible say to this issue? Can you, as a believer, lose fellowship with God based on your lifestyle?

David's experience as an Old Testament believer would answer that question with a "yes." In the early verses of Psalm 32, he reveals the anguish and deep conviction he felt when he refused to confess his sin to God. But then in verse 5 he writes, "I acknowledged my sin unto thee, and mine iniquity have I not hid. I said, I will confess my transgressions unto the LORD; and thou forgavest the iniquity of my sin. Selah."

---

7   Wayne A. Grudem, *Systematic Theology: An Introduction to Biblical Doctrine* (Grand Rapids, MI: Zondervan Academic, 1994), 740.

Incidentally, this verse provides a great definition of confession—the acknowledgment of sin. Confession is simply agreeing with God. It is not groveling before a judge, nor is it doing emotional penitence while pleading for a forgiveness God may choose to withhold. It is simply acknowledging that my sin is, in fact, sin. (Psalm 51:3, also a psalm of confession by David, expresses the same truth: "For I acknowledge my transgressions: and my sin is ever before me.")

We also see the need for a believer's confession of sin for restored fellowship with the Father in the New Testament. Specifically, we see it in the very context of 1 John 1:9 where three verses prior (verse 6), the question of whether you can lose fellowship with God based on your lifestyle is again answered with a definitive *yes:* "If we say that we have fellowship with him, and walk in darkness, we lie, and do not the truth." Verse 7 continues, "But if we walk in the light, as he is in the light, we have fellowship one with another, and the blood of Jesus Christ his Son cleanseth us from all sin."

Yet, in spite of this clarity, here are a couple quotes from radical grace teachers arguing that a Christian cannot lose fellowship with God:

> How can you be separated or have distance from someone who lives *in you?* The idea that we're out of fellowship with God when we do wrong is a lie. It's one of those clichés. It sounds good, but it's not biblical. There is nothing you can do to put yourself out of fellowship with God.[8]

> Fellowship with Him is not broken because our forgiveness is not contingent on what we do. It is contingent on the finished work of Jesus. We do not confess our sins to be forgiven. We confess or speak openly to our gracious Father because we have already been forgiven.[9]

---

8   Steve McVey, *52 Lies Heard in Church Every Sunday* (Eugene, OR: Harvest House Publishers, 2011), 73.
9   Joseph Prince, *Destined to Reign* (Tulsa, OK: Harrison House Publishers, 2007), 104.

To deny that sin affects our relationship with God is to treat it lightly and take God's grace for granted. It can lead to a license to live in sin. And, in some cases, it has led to some strange conclusions about God's chastisement and the convicting ministry of the Holy Spirit.

Part of the ministry of the Holy Spirit in our battle against sin is, of course, His convicting work in our hearts (John 16:8; Hebrews 12:5). Yet, radical grace teachers flatly deny this. Joseph Prince writes, "The bottom line is that the Holy Spirit never convicts you of your sins. He never comes to point out your faults."[10]

God *does* point out our sin, and He calls us to repentance and restoration. For example, Paul called the Corinthian believers to repentance through the epistle of 1 Corinthians, and in 2 Corinthians 7:8–10, he expressed his joy that they had indeed showed godly sorrow and repentance over their sin. In Revelation 2, Christ Himself called two different local churches to repent over specific sins—the church in Ephesus for leaving their first love (verses 4–5) and the church in Pergamos for tolerating false doctrine (verses 15–16).

Another expression of the Father's grace in our lives is His chastisement, as Hebrews 12 teaches us. As you might expect, radical grace teachers find this passage difficult since it plainly teaches God deals with His children over their present sin. (Again, our sin has been fully dealt with in terms of our sonship. It is, in fact, this sonship that causes God to bring chastisement into our lives.) The radical grace teacher has to really struggle to recast this passage, including suggesting that the writer of Hebrews originally wrote in Hebrew and mistranslated into Greek, so that the meaning of *scourge* (verse 6) means "to deeply enquire into."[11] In effect, they take away the obvious interpretation of the passage—that

---

10 Ibid., 134.
11 Robert Lightner, *Sin, the Savior, and Salvation* (Grand Rapids, MI: Kregel Publications, 1991), 268.

God chastens His children for their present sin in order to more fully develop the fruit of righteousness in them—to be able to support their teaching that if God were to deal with our present sin at all, He would be negating the righteousness of Christ. This completely overlooks the obvious and orthodox understanding of our position in Christ and its bearing on our progressive sanctification.

WHAT IS THE CONCERN?

So is all of this just splitting hairs over terms? After all, no one is saying we shouldn't grow spiritually or become more Christlike, right?

Issues surrounding grace are always doctrinally vital to understand. But I believe the trends we've looked at in this chapter are especially important for Baptist leaders for a few reasons:

We are to rightly divide the Word.

If something is not true, it is not helpful. Regardless of how sincere the motive may be that Christians not be held down by a legalistic bondage and that they be liberated to grace, if what the radical grace teachers write is not doctrinally true, it's not practically helpful.

In fact, in every instance that I read the quotes of radical grace teachers, I find, at best, a shallow understanding of biblical terms or, at worse, a deliberate mishandling of God's Word.

For example, read the quote below by Andrew Farley, which takes us back to 1 John 1:9. But here I want to look at it in the context of rightly dividing Scripture.

> There's still one big worm in the apple when it comes to understanding our unconditional forgiveness and cleansing: If we

confess our sin, he is faithful and just and will forgive us our sins and purify us from all unrighteousness (1 John 1:9). No other verse has caused more damage to Christians' assurance of their forgiveness. If we take that opening phrase out of context, our whole understanding of God's unconditional forgiveness can fall to pieces. It's all too easy to interpret this verse to mean that God responds, daily, to our confessions by doling out new portions of forgiveness and cleansing. God forgives us Christians only if we confess our sins, we might think. But this is not the context of 1 John 1:9.[12]

Quite honestly, I have a hard time getting past him saying, "No other verse has caused more damage." Although he goes on to say it is (in his opinion) the out-of-context application of it to which he is referring, he himself doesn't understand the context of 1 John, but imposes his definitions of forgiveness into the text. This kind of manipulating and manhandling Scripture to suit the authors' interpretations is all throughout Farley, Ellis, Prince, and McVey's writings. The writings of these authors often conflict with Scripture and are self-serving of the author's interpretations.

We are called to examine our lives and deal with sin.

Sin *does* affect our relationship with God.

God tells husbands in 1 Peter 3:7 that if they are living in a prideful or insensitive way toward their wives, their prayers could be hindered: "Likewise, ye husbands, dwell with them according to knowledge, giving honour unto the wife, as unto the weaker vessel, and as being heirs together of the grace of life; that your prayers be not hindered."

In 1 Corinthians 11:31–32, God commands us to "judge ourselves": "For if we would judge ourselves, we should not be judged. But when we are

---

12   Andrew Farley, *God Without Religion* (Grand Rapids, MI: Baker Books, 2011), 191.

judged, we are chastened of the Lord, that we should not be condemned with the world."

Teaching that points only to the imputed righteousness of Christ with no emphasis on obeying the commands of Christ limits believers from the joy of obedience. As Randy Alcorn said, "Any concept of grace that makes us feel more comfortable about sinning is not biblical grace. God's grace never encourages us to live in sin; on the contrary, it empowers us to say no to sin and yes to truth."[13]

Furthermore, if we ignore sin in our lives, we will miss out on the fellowship with the Father that He desires for us to enjoy.

We are to be conforming to the image of Christ.

The doctrine of progressive sanctification is not legalism. Progressive sanctification is taught in Romans 6–8 as we learn to have victory over sin and are assured that in God's foreknowledge and predetermined plan, we will be conformed to the image of Christ: "For whom he did foreknow, he also did predestinate to be conformed to the image of his Son, that he might be the firstborn among many brethren" (Romans 8:29). Sanctification consists of a daily realization that in Christ we have died and in Christ we are raised (Romans 6), that we still battle the flesh (Romans 7), and that God has given us the Holy Spirit to aid in the process of sanctification (Romans 8).

First John 3:2–3 assures us that this will take place in completion when we see Christ and tells us that this hope gives motivation now to be living holy lives: "Beloved, now are we the sons of God, and it doth not yet appear what we shall be: but we know that, when he shall appear, we shall

---

13   Randy Alcorn, *The Grace and Truth Paradox: Responding with Christlike Balance* (New York: Multnomah Books, 2003), 82.

be like him; for we shall see him as he is. And every man that hath this hope in him purifieth himself, even as he is pure."

When all you look at is the imputed righteousness of Christ, you miss the hope of progressive sanctification. God is conforming me to the image of Christ, and that is good news. "Being confident of this very thing, that he which hath begun a good work in you will perform it until the day of Jesus Christ" (Philippians 1:6).

CELEBRATE GRACE

Of all the terms prefaced by the word *hyper,* grace is my least favorite. That's because, as I already mentioned, grace is so amazing that it's not possible to have too much of it.

I want to experience *more* of God's grace. I want to become more gracious. I want to introduce more people to the amazing, life-changing grace of God.

But the best way to celebrate grace is not by misunderstanding it. It is by receiving it to live Christ's life in the power of the Holy Spirit.

CHAPTER TWELVE

GENERATIONAL TRENDS

DESPITE THE CONCERNS ADDRESSED in this book, when I survey today's ministry landscape, I'm encouraged.

Why?

First, I'm hopeful for revival. The fact that our culture is becoming increasingly hostile toward Christianity is disappointing, but Scripture warned us this would happen (2 Timothy 3:1–4). So I hope and pray for revival of God's people, which would certainly result in renewed evangelism and fruit. I believe that the world's antagonism toward Christ could be setting the stage for a great last days' revival.

Second, I'm encouraged because of the next generation of leaders who desire to see a great moving of God and have the faith to believe it could happen.

Millennials are no longer *tomorrow's* leaders. They are *today's* leaders. And soon, the same will be said of Generation Z.

Our society is currently made up of five generations:

- **Builders**—Traditionalists and the Silent Generation (born pre-1945)
- **Baby Boomers** (born 1946-1964)
- **Generation X** (born 1965-1979)
- **Generation Y**—The Millennials (born 1980-2001)
- **Generation Z**—The Post-Millennials (born 2001 onwards)[1]

Over the past couple years, I have been blessed by a refreshing meeting of preachers, organized by millennials, called the Standing Together Ministry Summit. The summits began in Fort Worth, Texas, to uphold the need to stand together with like-minded pastors for sharpening and encouraging. One of the blessings to me in these meetings has been that the organizers have emphasized the need for cross-generational fellowship and encouragement within a clearly-defined setting of doctrinal convictions.

If we who are baby boomers and older dismiss younger leaders because their paradigm is sometimes different than ours, or if we insist that they become just like us in order to serve alongside us, we miss their unique insights and strengths. Additionally, pastors of my age need a plan for succession and a plan to help younger pastors who are solid in doctrine to fill the pulpits of tomorrow. As William Vanderbloemen and Warren Bird note in their book *Next*, "Every pastor is an interim pastor of some sort."[2]

I began pastoring when I was twenty-four years old, and I have been pastoring what is considered a megachurch since I was thirty-four. For

---

1   Benjamin Windle, "Eight Innovations to Leading Millennials," www. millennialswhitepaper.com, (2016).
2   William Vanderbloemen and Warren Bird, *Next: Pastoral Succession That Works* (Grand Rapids, MI: Baker Publishing Group, 2014), chap. 1, Kindle.

the ten year period from when I began until our church surpassed two thousand in weekly attendance, I was the age of today's millennial.

Even back then, there were leaders who were dismissive, taking a "Let's wait and see how long he lasts" posture toward me and our ministry. But I remember with deep gratitude those who were encouraging and made an "I'm here to help you any way that I can" offer.

Regardless of our age, our ministry perspective should always be broader than one generation or even a comparison of generations. Our focus should be Christ, and our ministry criteria the New Testament. So, although we are looking at generational differences and trends in this chapter, my objective is that we would do so through a biblical perspective and with a Christ-centered focus.

With that said, what are the specific leanings of younger generations? And in what ways might these be developed or driven as a response to opposite leanings of prior generations?

ENCOURAGING EMPHASIS OF TODAY'S EMERGING LEADERS

Each generation has its strengths and weaknesses, for sure, but I love what I see in the strengths of leaders younger than me. And I have enjoyed listening to millennials who articulate these truths:

Desire for biblical preaching and teaching—There is a tremendous emphasis in today's leaders on *biblical* teaching and preaching. And I love this.

I'm thankful for how today's millennial pastors desire a return to theologically-rich messages and expository preaching that avoids hobby horses, soap boxes, and pet peeves. They have a desire to rightly divide

Scripture and a rejection of messages that mostly relate a preacher's experiences and counsel with a few proof texts thrown in.

In Paul's final letter to Timothy, he emphasized the importance of studying the Word of God thoroughly and preaching it regularly: "Study to shew thyself approved unto God, a workman that needeth not to be ashamed, rightly dividing the word of truth" (2 Timothy 2:15). "Preach the word; be instant in season, out of season; reprove, rebuke, exhort with all longsuffering and doctrine" (2 Timothy 4:2).

If we are to move forward for God in this day, it will be because God's people understand His Word—not just the doctrines of it, but the words themselves. Expository preaching and thorough biblical teaching are essential to this process.

Desire for Christ-centered ministry—In today's celebrity culture, millennial leaders are weary of man-promoting and instead desire to lift up Christ. They are conscious that *He* is the head of the church (Colossians 1:18). They want their preaching and every ministry of the local church to point people to Jesus.

Desire for emphasis on transformation through identification with Christ and fullness of the Spirit—Today's leaders know, sometimes from personal experience, that outside-in transformation doesn't work. They don't want young Christians to feel pressured into first conforming their lifestyles before being convinced biblically of truth. They believe the Holy Spirit regenerates us at the new birth and gives us a new heart (2 Corinthians 5:17). They want change to happen from the inside out as Christians understand who they are in Christ and yield to the commands of the Holy Spirit. This is the only kind of lasting change that brings real spiritual fruit that glorifies God.

Desire to work with others—For all the strengths of independent Baptists, there has been way too much infighting. Today's younger leaders are tired of pride, jealousy, and superfluous contention and just want to work with others to reach the world with the gospel. They are more concerned with making a difference than with getting the credit or with whose methods get used. I applaud this Philippians 1:27 spirit of "striving together for the faith of the gospel."

Desire for authentic ministry—Big services and special Sundays are awesome for the ways they motivate and mobilize a local church in reaching its community. But today's leaders want there to be an emphasis on the week-to-week local church functions that bring ongoing personal growth. They want Christians to see real life change—not just for churches to see single big Sundays or services. They want to impact lives—not just have a smooth-running Sunday program. They want authenticity, where the ultimate measure of effectiveness is change, not size; Christlikeness, not numeric growth.

An emphasis on grace as a motivator—Today's leaders are well-aware that pressure, guilt, and shame do not work as long-term motivators. They are also aware that grace is the God-given change agent and internal motivator that sustains Christian growth over the decades.

Desire to reach their generation—Although I love and appreciate my heritage, I also hunger for revival *today*. Today's pastors are well aware that if all they have to offer newly-saved Christians is other people's recollections of leaders they never met from the olden days, they don't have much. They want to be part of something great for God in *their* generation. They get frustrated when they sense defeatism over the changing culture and desire instead to truly impact this present culture.

I'm grateful for these biblical and hopeful traits I see among younger leaders. And I want to do everything I can to encourage them to take a bold stand for Christ and to reach their generation with the gospel.

CONCERNS FOR FUTURE DIRECTION

Before we look at some of the specific concerning trends, I want to highlight a general and generational progression I often see in emerging leaders who come from a conservative, separatist background of faith. We could picture this progression with the following chart:

Doctrinal Convictions
_____

Focus on Relevance
_____

Over Contextualization
_____

Change of Affiliations
_____

Compromise

Doctrinal conviction represents the starting place of the church in which a man was saved or matured in his faith and his pastor who has stood for truth and against compromise. As this young man then enters the ministry, he begins to pay attention to contextualizing truth (which is important). But sometimes, a leader shifts so that he becomes less concerned about convictions and has more of a **focus on relevance.** He still has the same doctrine, but what has captured his attention is the packaging or communication of it.

From there, it is a small step to **over contextualization.** And the more he becomes involved in over contextualizing, the less he feels comfortable with his home pastor or his early training. This naturally leads to a **change of affiliations** with others who feel similarly or perhaps who are outside the young leader's original ministry context altogether. At this point, the leader may have the same doctrine as he started with and may even still identify as an independent Baptist, but he has closer relationships with and is more greatly influenced by those in the final group than those who would align with where he started.

The great likelihood is that he will eventually **compromise** his early convictions related to both doctrine and practice and will become like those he has followed through the last few steps of this progression.

I share this progress because one's direction matters, sometimes more than one's specific position. There is a linkage between the changing of ministry "style" when it is accompanied with a changing of associations. And it often leads to a changing of doctrine. When I see independent Baptist pastors trying to prove they are "gospel-centered" and not "fearing men" while they invite men of different faith or practice to speak, I become concerned for the direction.

The final step of changing doctrine may not happen until the next generation. But when a leader throws caution to the wind concerning ministry input, places little emphasis on biblical holiness in worship, and abandons distinctions in separation, there does come a point where he will say, "I'm willing to cut off my heritage and follow another group." He may even feel hurt or misunderstood in the process.

So, how are some of these directional trends playing out currently? We could categorize them in a variety of ways, but here are five that I believe are indicative, not necessarily of compromise, but of directional concern. These, of course, don't represent every one of today's leaders, but I hope you'll read through them with an open heart to the Holy Spirit personally and an open mind to future direction generally.

Downplaying the importance of declarative, biblical preaching—I know that loud preaching is not necessarily good preaching. Just because someone says something forcefully doesn't make them right or necessarily more likely to be heard. So I'm not talking here about preaching that is a loud declaration of personal ideas. But there can be no replacement for the biblical declaring of God's truth through preaching. Be careful that you "Despise not prophesyings" (1 Thessalonians 5:20) but that preaching is a central aspect of your local church worship and gospel ministry.

Lack of appreciation for heritage—I'm grieved by the tendency that is common today to castigate all conservative leaders, especially those from previous generations, as narrow-minded or pharisaical. This is simply not true. I know that my mentors had their weaknesses. But I also saw their strengths firsthand. It's easy several decades later to look back and criticize areas of weakness, but let's not fail to appreciate their solid convictions and courage to stand for truth in difficult days.

This tendency is not unique to independent Baptists; it's human nature. In fact, I see it in the Southern Baptist Convention by young men who lack appreciation for the sacrifices made by those who turned the convention back to a stand for biblical doctrine.

Beware of a vantage point on your heritage that doesn't see and appreciate the good and that doesn't acknowledge the doctrinal and directional benefits you have received from those who have gone before you. Proverbs 27:10 cautions, "Thine own friend, and thy father's friend, forsake not."

Among independent Baptists, I see young church planters who gladly take missions support from the previous generation while telling them how much they appreciate them. But in reality, they are shifting in their ministry philosophy from their mentors, and after they have raised support, will unveil a church launch that bears little resemblance to how they were trained and how they represented themselves. This is not only a lack of appreciation; it is also a lack of honesty. Dr. Don Sisk recently said of one such church planter, "He is raising support under false pretenses." This doesn't mean you have to hold every method your sending pastor held. But it does mean you should be honest about your ministry philosophy and the general methods you plan to use.

Sometimes over the course of time and through the ministry of the Holy Spirit that leads us to make mid-course adjustments, we look back on our earliest days of ministry and see a glaring need for growth. This is good and needed. But don't let those periods of adjustment lead you to "outgrow" those who invested in you so that you look on them with disdain or pity. Truly, these responses are marks of immaturity.

I think of the grief that the apostle Paul felt when those whom he had led to Christ and discipled in the faith, in effect, turned from his teaching and even turned on him, thinking of him as an adversary. He wrote, "Where is then the blessedness ye spake of? for I bear you record, that, if it had been possible, ye would have plucked out your own eyes, and have given them to me. Am I therefore become your enemy, because I tell you the truth?" (Galatians 4:15–16).

Uplifting authors and pastors with doctrinal and ecumenical weaknesses—When I was in my twenties, I heard a well-known fundamental leader tell preachers attending a conference that they should only read books by fundamentalists within a certain circle that was close to him. Honestly, that's ridiculous. I know what he was getting at (because I talked with him about it after the message): he didn't want undiscerning people to be pulled away from Bible convictions by authors who were antagonistic toward fundamentalism. But I believe a spiritual leader should be discerning enough to be able to eat the meat and spit out the bones. And if we're not helping young leaders develop that kind of discernment, it probably doesn't reflect favorably on our own leadership.

That said, however, there is a difference between reading a book and uplifting an author or teacher. Although I read widely, I do my best to read discerningly, and I promote sparingly. Occasionally, I'll give a book to the men on our staff for reading and group discussion that might not be written by an author I could easily promote without a disclaimer. But when we discuss it, we bring up the issues with which we disagree as well as looking for what we can use and implement. This is different than a blanket endorsement through a quote on social media that is seen by people at all levels of growth in spiritual discernment.

I am aware that some of this distinction may be generational. Where I am slow to reference authors who are known for variant doctrine or practice, a younger leader isn't as likely to see a mention as an endorsement. But I do believe care needs to be taken. Even in this book, I have tried to distance myself from false doctrine when quoting from those authors in an area of agreement.

But there is another level of concern, and that has to do with our own perceptions of other authors.

Everyone looks better in print or on the internet. There is a tendency to read other authors and, in seeing their spiritual journey through only their eyes, compare it to others' spiritual journey through your eyes. Pretty soon, authors from almost every other sphere of Christendom have a better understanding of grace, the gospel, and ministry than anyone you already know. But what is easy to forget is that those closest to these other authors are sometimes seeing every *other* circle the same way. So, don't be oblivious to the fact that just as we independent Baptists have our weaknesses, so authors and leaders in other groups do as well.

When Baptists who are moving leftward start their "journey," they often begin to quote much "smarter" authors whom they invite into their lives as mentors. Since I began this project ten years ago, however, several of these "much more spiritual" authors have left the ministry in disgrace. It's really best not to compare our worst to their best and to remember that their best (like ours) has a worse side.

Promoting conferences that are ecumenical in nature—This goes back to the doctrinal side of separation. I don't see myself feeling comfortable in a conference that promotes Charismatic doctrine, ecumenicalism, continuationism, social gospel, alcohol consumption, and says these doctrines are secondary for the sake of furthering the gospel.

As a pastor, I have a genuine concern that to attend and promote an ecumenical conference on Saturday and then to preach on separation on Sunday would be confusing to my church family. The Saturday hashtag with a picture and quote of a conference speaker at whose church I could not in good conscience preach says to my church, "There is no distinction or difference between what this speaker or denomination believes and the doctrine we preach." As Paul told the church at Corinth, "For if the trumpet give an uncertain sound, who shall prepare himself to the battle?" (1 Corinthians 14:8). We should recognize Christian liberty in this area, but a visit to a conference can become a continuing identification which changes one's direction of ministry.

Dismissing personal separation—While good Christians will vary in the exact ways of living out a sanctified life, there should be no room for belittling the need for personal holiness.

Ephesians 5:8–10 instructs us to "walk as children of light . . . Proving what is acceptable unto the Lord." Part of the way that we exercise discernment *(proving)* to live a lifestyle *(walk)* as children of the light is by deriving personal guidelines from specific Bible commands and principles that help us avoid sin and point others to Christ.

As leaders in ministry, we also may set leadership requirements for those who are helping to mature others in their faith. Whether it be for our own lives or in establishing guidelines for ministry leaders, the process should begin with Jesus and have a goal of pointing others to Him as well.

Start with Jesus. Spend time with Him in His Word.

Understand a Bible command. A command is obvious. It is a spelled out instruction in the Word of God: "But as he which hath called you is holy, so be ye holy in all manner of conversation; Because it is written, Be ye holy; for I am holy" (1 Peter 1:15–16).

Draw a principle from that command. Bible principles allow us to address the specific issues of life that are addressed in a larger sense in Scripture. For instance, from 1 Peter 1:15–16 (as well as many other passages), we draw the principle of holiness which we could state as, "My lifestyle is to reflect the holiness of God and should be separated from ungodliness."

Set guidelines. From a principle, we develop *standards* or *guidelines* that bring the original command into direct contact with our daily living. From the principle of holiness, we could develop specific personal standards related to music, relationships, entertainment, and more.

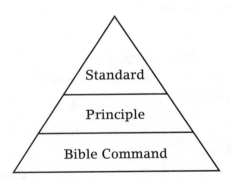

The point is that these guidelines should be firmly attached to a Bible principle. Also, because these guidelines are not specifically spelled out in Scripture, we must rely on the leading of the Holy Spirit for our own lives and give grace to other Christians who draw their lines differently.

We must remember the ultimate purpose here is the glory of God and the furtherance of His gospel.

Christian institutions, such as Christian schools and Bible colleges, have to set some of these guidelines arbitrarily in the form of rules for the sake of safety and conformability. For instance, our Christian school has a rule that boys' hair must be off their ears and collars. The principle behind it comes from 1 Corinthians 11:14, "Doth not even nature itself teach you, that, if a man have long hair, it is a shame unto him?" From this verse, we know that a man should not have long hair, but exactly how long is *long* is not in the text. So we arbitrarily set a guideline for our school while doing our best to teach our students, not only the guideline, but the principle behind it.

It's worth noting here that the secular world also encourages the development of personal standards. Rather than rooting these in biblical principle, however, they are rooted in personal values or mission. Read almost any secular book on productivity or life fulfillment, and you'll find that it begins with the importance of developing personal values and living according to them. How much more should we, who have the only and ultimate standard of objective truth in the Word of God, work to align our daily lives to it in specific and practical ways?

THE FINE ART OF CORRECTION

Often, the present generation overlooks the strengths and sees only the weaknesses of the past generation. The result can be an overcorrection that simply veers from one ditch to the opposing ditch.

When we see an imbalance in a previous generation and, through the ministry of the Holy Spirit, seek to make a biblical correction, we have the opportunity to end up with a stronger, more biblical position than before. These kinds of mid-course adjustments are necessary in all of our lives and ministries. But when we see an imbalance and, out of frustration or disillusionment, make a correction in a reactionary (rather than a biblical and causative) way, we usually overcorrect.

The following chart illustrates how this works. The column on the left lists some of the imbalances I have heard leaders share they have felt. The center column lists the desire a leader may have to correct a previous imbalance or concern. And the far right column shows the danger of overcorrection.

Imbalance	Correction	Danger of Overcorrection
Trained in autocratic churches	Want less dogma and more discussion	Giving up the authority of Scripture and the commands to preach and to contend for the faith
Heard only topical messages	Want minds challenged	Intellectual elitism
Forced to sing boring music	Want to express true passion	Employing rock and roll music in church
Given lists of rules as a measure of holiness	Want emphasis on Christ's transformation from within	Not leading people to set personal boundaries of protection
Heard sinners condemned harshly	Want humble preaching that acknowledges the depth of depravity in all sin	Not warning a flock of dangers of specific sins
Watched petty divisions within the movement of fundamentalism	Want greater emphasis on unity	Disregarding commands for biblical separation

This list is just a sample. But I hope it gives you a visual of the importance of making mid-course adjustments carefully and biblically.

It's not that you can ever overpractice truth. Truth is truth. The danger in overcorrecting comes when a leader fails to consider the multiple aspects of truth that relate to a particular area. Thus, rather than simply correcting an imbalance, he reacts. The reality is that, as in driving, accidents can be just as serious on either side of the road.

A FEW WORDS OF ADVICE

I feel myself to be in a unique age as it relates to generational stereotypes. I'm a young baby boomer but on the edge of Generation X. My communication defaults are more old school partially because my mentors were and partially because I developed most of my personal preferences before the age of the internet. But I share younger generations' passion for creativity and collaboration toward common goals. I watch some older leaders shut down or shut out younger leaders because the older feel threatened or disrespected, and I watch younger leaders disregard the opportunity to learn from older because the younger feel misunderstood or judged.

In the next few paragraphs, I'd like to share six suggestions—important to every generation—that can work as guardrails against overcorrecting as we move forward in seeking to follow the leadership of the Holy Spirit. For older leaders, these guardrails give credibility and opportunity to invest. For younger leaders, they give protection and opportunity to develop needful relationships.

Exercise a loving spirit. It's easy for us to see the lack of love we perceive others showing toward us. But sometimes our own interactions with others are motivated by something less than love. "By this shall

all men know that ye are my disciples, if ye have love one to another" (John 13:35).

Build vibrant churches. Our goal should be to build a church that honors Christ and is actively and proactively reaching our world with the gospel.

Leaders who develop a kind of bunker mentality of just trying to "hold on until the rapture" should not be surprised if younger leaders who want to change the world with the gospel are not attracted to their ministry philosophy.

Conversely, churches that appear vibrant because of loud music and trendy use of technology are not, in fact, vibrant spiritually if they are not seeing people saved, baptized, and lives changing in conformity to the image of Christ. The Laodicean church of Revelation 3 was undoubtedly one of modern appeal, but it didn't have Christ. If you lead such a church, you should not be offended if older ministry mentors question your ministry methods.

Be cautious and positive on social media. A pastor can know his heritage by the church name on his ordination certificate; he can know his current ministry philosophy by his social media posts and feed. Use social media to build up, not to tear down. It doesn't hurt to promote conservative quotes and authors. And certainly, use it to encourage your own church family in the work of the Lord.

Have older mentors. Every generation needs the one preceding and the one following. Paul needed to pass the baton to Timothy; Timothy needed the mentoring of Paul.

If you are young enough to know leaders fifteen and twenty years beyond you in ministry, value their input. Sometimes I'll see a snide remark from younger pastors, graduates of various conservative Bible colleges, related to not seeking the approval of their alma mater or other preachers. These kinds of comments sadden me. Not only am I grieved that they feel the need to defend themselves, but I'm also grieved that they would feel defensive toward those who have significantly invested in their ministry.

In addition to welcoming the influence of older mentors in your life, it is important also to be discerning of those who desire to influence you through their online presence, but who don't believe or practice the same as you do. I appreciate the ability to get spiritual encouragement from others on the Internet, and I strive to give it as well. The danger comes when someone uses these sources of input as a replacement for their local church pastor or for the input of godly mentors who can speak far more personally into their lives. Sadly, the major influencers on Christian television and social media are modeling ministry styles that are not biblically sound. These outside influencers can draw a sincere leader away from clarity in their ministry philosophy and even from the gospel itself. Throughout the epistle of Galatians, Paul questioned the believers, not about *what* pulled them away from truth, but about *who* pulled them away. (See Galatians 3:1, 5:7.) Don't allow anyone to—by direct counsel, inadvertent influence, or hoped-for acceptance—pull you away from the truth.

When I was younger in ministry, I needed to hear more about finding acceptance and validation in Christ alone. Today, however, I'm hearing more of younger pastors being challenged to follow after and seek counsel either from their own peers or "only Jesus" so they are not trapped by seeking the validation of others.

This counsel actually feeds into the validation trap, only it perpetuates the cycle from the other side. Here's how it works:

A young leader looks to men instead of to Christ for validation and acceptance. (To be fair, we should note that this is not always the fault of the mentors; sometimes it is just due to the natural bent of our human heart to look for fulfillment outside of Christ.) For a while, he receives this validation; but over time, he finds it was hollow.

By this time, however, he's been in ministry long enough to influence younger leaders himself. With a heart perhaps disappointed in past relationships, he swings the pendulum of counsel the opposite direction and says, "Don't follow men; only follow Jesus." If you read between the lines, what this counsel really means is, "Don't follow *them;* follow *me*—I understand how to give you validation without insisting you do ministry their way."

What follows is a new cycle of young men still seeking validation and approval, just from another set of leaders.

Beware of this trap. Seek the counsel of older mentors, but don't seek to find acceptance that has already been given to you in Christ.

Seek solid preaching. Books, seminars, and TED Talks have their place. But seek out preaching—biblical, Christ-centered, Holy Spirit-filled preaching.

Listen to it on podcasts. Hear it with an open heart through guest preachers. Study God's Word and expound it in your own pulpit. Preaching has no replacement in the local church.

Fellowship with likeminded men from various ages and backgrounds. There are good, godly men across America who still uphold Baptist distinctives and sound doctrine. Don't isolate yourself into one independent Baptist clique, whether that be those from your alma mater or those who are against your alma mater. Seek out fellowship with those older than you, younger than you, laboring in different places than you . . . those who love God, love the local church, and are likeminded because they are biblically centered.

A TARGET LARGER THAN ONE GENERATION

God has given us an incredible trust—the gospel of Jesus Christ (1 Timothy 1:11).

Your ministry and my ministry isn't about you or me. It's not even about your generation or my generation. It is about Jesus, preaching His gospel, and pleasing Him who is the head of the church.

Yes, sometimes to accomplish these goals, it helps us to step back and understand the dynamics of various generations and trends within them. But ultimately, our purpose must not be to please a particular generation or attract church attenders of a decade-year range.

Our goal is to please Jesus who is "Alpha and Omega, the beginning and the ending . . . which is, and which was, and which is to come, the Almighty" (Revelation 1:8). "Unto *him* be glory in the church by Christ Jesus throughout all ages, world without end. Amen" (Ephesians 3:21).

PART THREE

REACHING FORWARD
WITH THE GOSPEL

CHAPTER THIRTEEN

SOLDIERS AND BUILDERS

I N THE 1865 PREMIER ISSUE of Charles Spurgeon's periodical, *The Sword and the Trowel,* he developed the reasoning behind its name: "We would ply the Trowel with untiring hand for the building up of Jerusalem's dilapidated walls, and wield the Sword with vigour and valour against the enemies of the Truth."[1]

The reference is to Nehemiah 4:17–18 where the Israelites rebuilt the walls of Jerusalem. Because they were under constant threat of attack, they built with one hand and held their swords ready with the other: "They which builded on the wall, and they that bare burdens, with those that laded, every one with one of his hands wrought in the work, and with the other hand held a weapon. For the builders, every one had his

---

1   Charles Haddon Spurgeon, Susannah Spurgeon, and Joseph Harrald, *The Autobiography of Charles H. Spurgeon: 1856-1878* (Chicago: F. H. Revell, 1899), 308.

sword girded by his side, and so builded . . . ." It is with this spirit and diligence that I want to "earnestly contend for the faith which was once delivered unto the saints" (Jude 3) as well as labor "together with God" (1 Corinthians 3:9).

The New Testament instructs us to be both soldiers (Ephesians 6:13, 2 Timothy 2:3, 1 Peter 1:13) and builders (1 Corinthians 3:11–13, Ephesians 2:19–21, Jude 20). Many of today's compromises over truth and ridiculous infighting are the result of being one without the other. Too often, we make the type of issues that we have discussed in these chapters more about personalities and preferences than about truth or building. Our goal must remain to contend for the faith while laboring with Christ to build His church.

But how do we do this? How do we find the balance of laboring with one hand and contending with the other? In these next few pages, I'd like to tie together the various topics we've addressed with a few overriding principles that should govern our approach to contemporary theology and our practice of biblical separation.

WALK IN HUMILITY

The gospel and the reality of Christ's sacrifice for us should create humility, not pride. James 4:6 tells us, "But he giveth more grace. Wherefore he saith, God resisteth the proud, but giveth grace unto the humble."

We need humility to search out trends and their underlying theology before either giving a rebuttal or jumping on a bandwagon.

A weakness of my generation has been the quick answer, "Because I said so." Or, "Because that's how we've always done it." We've had too much of a tendency to defend issues but miss the biblical principles behind them. When the issues shift, we retain a contending stance, but since there is no longer a real issue to contend for, we are then simply contentious. We need patient humility to listen and try to understand.

I would encourage all of us to have a heart that is pliable and willing to listen. Any of us can develop a spirit of pride that doesn't allow for growth or invite ongoing conversation.

We cultivate humility at the cross. It is there that "the love of Christ constraineth us" (2 Corinthians 5:14) and the gospel becomes our deepest motivation.

I appreciated a blog post that Kevin Folger wrote along these lines. He described an independent Baptist preachers fellowship where he had recently preached in which there were pastors and Christian workers from a variety of ages and perhaps styles and opinions.

> At this meeting there were some younger men I am sure that see things about ministry a bit differently than I do. I am not talking about Biblical doctrine, but more of preferences when it comes to ministry. As an older pastor, I may not agree with their preferences or want to practice them. Yet, if it isn't a Biblical mandate, then I must give them the right to allow the Holy Spirit to direct them. We don't have to agree on every issue to be friends and have fellowship. I want to go on record that I will use my influence and speak my mind about what I believe is the truth from the Word of God, but not everyone has to see everything just the way I do in other matters to be a friend or someone I can fellowship with.[2]

Allowing for differences in opinion and preferences is a sign of a humble spirit. Attempting to force uniformity across all churches and ministries is a sign of pride.

---

2   Kevin Folger, "Proud to Be an Independent Baptist!," *Cleveland Baptist Church*, May 25, 2018, http://clevelandbaptist.org/2018/05/proud-to-bean-independent-baptist.

We must be careful of assuming we know the motives of others. You may not agree with someone's method, but don't attack his motive. In my subjective analysis, 99 percent of the time when I hear pastors criticizing the motives of another pastor, they are speaking out of jealousy.

At the same time, however, when it comes to our own motives, we must be careful to maintain a teachable and humble spirit. I see two groups of preachers who are employing newer methods. There are those with an anti-anyone-who-doesn't-agree-with-me spirit. They interpret disagreement as a personal rejection and pull away from previous mentors who question them on their methods. Then there are those with a humble spirit who, even as they seek to employ new ideas to reach the lost with the gospel, keep a tender heart toward previous mentors and listen to the concerns they raise.

There are men whom I love deeply who use methods with which I strongly disagree. But I don't want to presume to know that their motive or their heart is wrong. I can study God's Word and use and promote methods and philosophies which I believe are biblical. I can't know someone else's heart.

As I mentioned earlier, some of what happens under the label of "separation" is downright ridiculous. Romans 14:10 puts silly issues of separation into perspective: "But why dost thou judge thy brother? or why dost thou set at nought thy brother? for we shall all stand before the judgment seat of Christ."[3] As Baptists, we believe in soul liberty—that each person is accountable to God. Ridiculous practices of separation that make us judges of one another do not advance the cause of biblical separation.

---

3   In *The Road Ahead*, I devoted a full chapter to Romans 14 and the importance of giving grace to one another.

Consider Luke 9 where the disciples, after arguing about which of them was the greatest, forbad someone who was casting out demons in Christ's name "because he followeth not with us" (Luke 9:49). Jesus' answer is instructive: "Forbid him not: for he that is not against us is for us." I have no desire to be someone who goes around forbidding others in their ministry practice because they don't do it just like me. The fact that God uses any of us is a miracle of His grace. But silly attacks on one another boil down to pride. Proverbs 13:10 nails it: "Only by pride cometh contention . . . ."

This pride manifests itself in jealousy, spite, and envy. James denounces it in strong language: "But if ye have bitter envying and strife in your hearts, glory not, and lie not against the truth. This wisdom descendeth not from above, but is earthly, sensual, devilish. For where envying and strife is, there is confusion and every evil work" (James 3:14–16).

In all honesty, this pride and bickering is not a fundamentalism issue so much as it is a human issue. You'll find it in every group, just over different issues. Some men take pride in their standards, others in their interpretations of grace. May we learn to simply glory in the cross. "But God forbid that I should glory, save in the cross of our Lord Jesus Christ, by whom the world is crucified unto me, and I unto the world" (Galatians 6:14).

BE CLEAR IN THE USE OF TRENDS AND TERMS

If you're a soldier or a builder, words matter. For a soldier, they could be a matter of life and death. For a builder, they could be the difference between a desired or undesired outcome. Yet, sometimes Christian leaders throw terms around without a clear understanding of their meanings.

This happens often with the term *emergent*. Although this word has been used so broadly that it is tough to pin down a single definition, it refers to real apostasy as people deny the basic truths of Scripture and even the authority of Scripture itself. When people use the term *emergent* as a social media grenade against someone who believes the same doctrine they believe but uses a different color of lights in a special service, it's frustrating and almost impossible to have a meaningful exchange of conversation.

Whatever the term may be, if we wrench words from their definitions and begin hurling them as accusations rather than using them in substantive conversation, we may as well not use terms at all.

ADJUST ONLY AS THE HOLY SPIRIT LEADS YOU

Be cautious about making wide-sweeping changes to your ministry philosophy. Don't make changes based on reading a single book or attending a single seminar. And don't make them without getting input from trusted mentors in ministry.

At the same time, however, do make changes as you grow in your walk with the Lord, your understanding of His Word, and your experience in ministry. Allow the Holy Spirit to continue to transform your life and mature your leadership through the power of the gospel.

It has been said that there are three times we experience spiritual breakthrough:

- When we hurt enough that we have to
- When we learn enough that we want to
- When we receive enough that we are able to

Sometimes all three of these work together as a season of suffering in our lives causes us to seek spiritual answers.

Remember, however, that not all change represents a spiritual breakthrough. The challenge for all of us is to recognize that during seasons of suffering and disappointment, we are more vulnerable to introspection and more likely to make unwise decisions. These are the very times when instead of questioning everything we've believed, we should go back to God's Word to anchor our beliefs and convictions more solidly in truth.

Over the years, I've observed two responses to seasons of difficulty that shape the future of someone's ministry. The first becomes a progression to ineffective ministry, while the second becomes a progression to more effective ministry.

The chart on the following pages contrasts both paths. The first progression accounts for far too many cases of pastors making poor ministry choices, changing their doctrinal persuasion, or substantially realigning and shifting their ministry philosophy. Notice how our response to hurts can be the determining difference in which path we take. The key in both of these scenarios is our response to pain—does it cause us to look within (to ourselves) and without (to those who failed us), or does it cause us to look up to the only One who can heal us?

PROGRESSION TO
INEFFECTIVE MINISTRY

1. Serving in awe—New in ministry, all of us are in awe of the opportunity of sharing the gospel and seeing it change lives.

2. Struggling in trials—A setback, lack of growth in ministry, season of suffering, relational misunderstanding, the sinful choices of a mentor, or deep personal disappointment comes into our lives.

3. Hurting—We hurt, grieve, and reach for comfort.

4. Searching—Sensing our inadequacy to deal with the pain, we question our ministry philosophy, perhaps even doctrine. We wonder if it was a flawed belief system that contributed to our pain. We may feel (either in reality or by perception) that we were involved in a ministry with a type of performance-based acceptance. And we may even become embittered by the cutting or shallow responses of others who share our current philosophy.

5. Realigning—We realign our beliefs and affiliations hoping to avoid future pain.

6. Changing—We change our ministry philosophy to match our new beliefs and affiliations, possibly even to gain the approval of our newly-chosen mentors.

7. Judging—We look down on those who invested in us in the past, now esteeming them to be either shallow, unbiblical, or unloving. Unconsciously, we also become unloving and ungraceful toward them . . . and our capacity and effectiveness in serving others diminishes.

PROGRESSION TO INCREASED
EFFECTIVENESS IN MINISTRY

1. Serving in awe—New in ministry, all of us are in awe of the opportunity of sharing the gospel and seeing it change lives.

2. Struggling in trials—A setback, lack of growth in ministry, season of suffering, relational misunderstanding, the sinful choices of a mentor, or deep personal disappointment comes into our lives.

3. Hurting—We hurt, grieve, and reach for comfort.

4. Searching—Sensing our inadequacy to deal with the pain, we go deeper into God's Word and discover resources of grace we didn't know existed. We may question our previous assumptions and beliefs, but these questions drive us to Christ and to Scripture and help us sort out assumption from belief.

5. Deepening—Our understanding of God, grace, and Scripture deepens, and our capacity to understand others' pain and bring biblical comfort enlarges.

6. Adjusting—Where our own pain has exposed faulty beliefs, assumptions, or philosophies, we adjust. Inasmuch as our previous ministry philosophy was aligned with Scripture, we maintain the whole, but willingly adjust the parts that need realignment.

7. Rejoicing—We rejoice in the healing God brings and in the enlarged opportunities for ministry.

Invariably, there will come times in all of our lives when we need to make mid-course adjustments. And often, God allows seasons of pain to set these adjustments in motion. My encouragement to you is to let the needed adjustments be just that—adjustments, not a complete overhaul of doctrine or ministry philosophy. "But the God of all grace, who hath called us unto his eternal glory by Christ Jesus, after that ye have suffered a while, make you perfect, stablish, strengthen, settle you" (1 Peter 5:10).

BUY THE TRUTH, AND SELL IT NOT

As we consider the issues of contemporary theology, remember that these are about something far greater than personal preferences or personalities. This is about truth itself. You and I are charged by God to be good soldiers who contend for the faith while at the same time being servant-leaders who partner with Christ in building up the body of Christ.

So yes, be creative in finding ways to get the gospel out. Be gospel-centered in your preaching and teaching. Be loving to others. But don't let go of the truth or your commitment to stand for it.

Don't be afraid to contend for the faith or separate from false doctrine or practice. Be diligent with your trowel, but don't be afraid to keep your sword in the other hand. You will need both to keep the faith for a lifetime.

CHAPTER FOURTEEN

STRENGTHEN THE THINGS WHICH REMAIN

I F WE LEARN ANYTHING from first-century churches—especially those churches in Asia Minor to which Christ sent letters through the pen of the Apostle John—it is the propensity of Christians, churches, and spiritual movements toward decline. This is why Christ commanded the church at Sardis, "Be watchful, and strengthen the things which remain . . ." (Revelation 3:2).

The good news is that the truth will always remain (Matthew 16:18), and the Holy Spirit is always speaking. Neither are bound by the level of our fervor or the correctness of our practices. They are eternal.

Yet, have you ever noticed that a second or third generation Christian may not fully appreciate or "own" the doctrine and maintain the fervor of previous generations? A man or woman is saved as an adult and freed from old habits and living. Their gratitude knows no bounds, and they gladly live the rest of their days with the desire to glorify the Lord. Their children or grandchildren, however, who are saved at a young age may not follow the Lord with the same spiritual fervor. To them, Christianity was more of a culture than a choice. They may indeed love the Lord, but they sometimes do so without the passionate gratitude of the previous generation.

If this is true in families, it is also true in ministries. The result is that churches that were once passionate for the faith may lose the fervency of their convictions. Some Baptists whose heritage was entrenched in soulwinning and personal sanctification now consider these topics to be nonintellectual. As they seek a new identity and new circles of fellowship, they willingly pull away even from the name *Baptist.*

Biblical ministry today faces challenges from within and without. From without, we face the challenges of a corrupt culture, biased media, and influence via the internet that is neither biblical nor proven. From within, we face the challenges of lukewarm Christianity, the passing away of strong, biblical leaders, a lack of evangelistic fervor, and hyper-critical men who create unnecessary divisions.

But I believe these challenges can be overcome. I want to encourage you, rather than abandoning the doctrine of separation or your Baptist heritage, strengthen it. Strengthen what is biblical, holy, and effective.

If pettiness among brothers discourages you, reach out to someone in love and encouragement.

If lack of cultural engagement frustrates you, hold a barbecue for your police force, encourage foster parents, offer oil changes for single moms.

If a lack of gospel focus in sanctification concerns you, preach the gospel for sanctification in your church.

If a disconnect between older and younger leaders frustrates you, reach out to someone outside of your generation to encourage or ask for counsel.

I don't make these suggestions dismissively, but to challenge you to be what you want to see in others.

Allow me to conclude this book with a recap of five vital convictions for today's ministry:

OUR CONVICTION FOR SOULWINNING

I've mentioned it already, but fervency in soulwinning is one of the strongest aspects of our history as independent Baptists. I so appreciate the compassionate fervor that was taught to me regarding having sustained, organized soulwinning outreach with a definitive strategy to reach a community with the gospel.

I'm thankful for the compassion for souls many of my early mentors modeled as they regularly, faithfully, and fervently shared the gospel in personal encounters and scheduled times of soulwinning. My wife, Terrie, was reached with the gospel by a compassionate bus worker who brought her to church. Compassionate, confrontational soulwinning is all but lost in much of Christendom, but it is needed now more than ever.

We so easily get our priorities skewed. We rejoice in visits to our websites, retweets of our social media content, and high numbers of attendance at our events. What Heaven rejoices over is one sinner who comes to faith in Christ (Luke 15:10).

If you read any secular book on purpose or corporate success, it will tell you that you must keep laser focus on your mission. The church is no corporation, but it can quickly lose its missional moorings and begin to drift. Without worship of Christ and obedient focus on His command, we drift. Interestingly, both worship and witness are addressed in Matthew's account of the Great Commission:

Then the eleven disciples went away into Galilee, into a mountain where Jesus had appointed them. And when they saw him, they worshipped him: but some doubted. And Jesus came and spake unto them, saying, All power is given unto me in heaven and in earth. Go ye therefore, and teach all nations, baptizing them in the name of the Father, and of the Son, and of the Holy Ghost: Teaching them to observe all things whatsoever I have commanded you: and, lo, I am with you alway, even unto the end of the world. Amen.

—MATTHEW 28:16–20

Nothing is as compelling as a church alive with new believers. A church where the gospel is at work will encourage every spiritual Christian in any generation.

OUR CONVICTION FOR ECCLESIASTICAL SEPARATION

As I have mentioned, one of the great areas of potential I see in today's younger leaders is their desire for unity. But as Oswald Chambers wisely observed, "Unguarded strength is double weakness."[1] While a desire for biblical unity is a tremendous attribute—and something that our movement greatly needs—there is a danger of it morphing into a desire for peace and union. Unity is based on shared truth; union may be based on shared compromise.

Spiritual leaders are careful to recognize the stewardship of their influence, and they work to protect those who may be weaker in the faith from mixed signals. As a pastor, I do not want to offend the conscience

---

1   Oswald Chambers, *My Utmost for His Highest* (New York: Dodd, Mead, and Company, 1985), 110.

of a younger or weaker Christian, and I don't want to build a bridge over which others may walk to unbiblical doctrine. Acts 20:28 instructs, "Take heed therefore unto yourselves, and to all the flock, over the which the Holy Ghost hath made you overseers, to feed the church of God, which he hath purchased with his own blood." Since the church is purchased and owned by Jesus, I must use wisdom and exercise discernment in whom I invite to preach in our pulpit.

I encourage pastors to weigh the influence of a guest speaker, blogger, or author upon their personal life and upon the life of the flock where they serve. As we think of the strengths and weaknesses of potential guests, we could consider what we may unintentionally endorse by inviting the guest.

For instance, you may be considering inviting a skilled apologist who has a great testimony of salvation who you hope will encourage your church family in the factual reliability of their faith. But if that same apologist believes in theistic evolution or is critical of soulwinning on social media, might that not also sow seed of doubt in members' minds, where you hoped to plant seeds of faith? Your desire for collaboration, if bought at the expense of separation, could actually bring confusion in the church.

I am cautious about whom I have in our pulpit. Yes, I wish there was greater collaboration in our ranks, but my main concern is the local flock. The conviction of early fundamentalists and Baptists was that doctrine determined fellowship. We must not only hold to truth, but we must contend for it: "Beloved . . . it was needful for me to write unto you, and exhort you that ye should earnestly contend for the faith which was once delivered unto the saints" (Jude 3). To promote on our church or social platforms men who deny or twist biblical truth is the opposite of our calling. Be careful then that in your desire for fellowship and gospel partnership you don't over collaborate and end up of a different doctrinal persuasion or dismissing the biblical ministry philosophy you've been taught.

I recently was speaking with a young leader from our own state of California about this subject, and he expressed his concern over it as well. His words were that he fears that the current spirit of collaboration among some of the younger leaders could become the seeds for the next generation of new evangelicalism. Some are even now, in fact, refusing to consider the reality that ministry influence from those of doctrinal differences is even a concern. I am not advocating the type of subjective rabble rousing that alienates good men over petty issues. I am talking about biblical holiness, the doctrine of salvation, the Word of God, creation, and eternal security.

My challenge to you is to hold to the truth and fellowship with those who do. Truth is never worth compromise. Hold it fast. Study, preach, and live sound doctrine: "Holding fast the faithful word as he hath been taught, that he may be able by sound doctrine both to exhort and to convince the gainsayers" (Titus 1:9). Don't dismiss biblical separation. It is still a vital part of the Christian life, and we need to practice it as much now as we ever did.

OUR CONVICTION FOR PURITY

Romans 14:16 warns, "Let not then your good be evil spoken of." Obviously, this is a needed warning because God included it in the Bible, but I think it's especially needful for us today.

The reality is that as independent Baptists, our good has often been evil spoken of . . . and sometimes because of our stupidity. I remember several years back when ABC ran a news story chronicling abuse allegations in independent Baptist churches. Although there were aspects of the report that felt like biased journalism, I knew some of it was most likely true. I was grieved for the victims and saddened by spiritual leaders who had abused their positions, hurt lambs, and "given great occasion to the enemies of the LORD to blaspheme" (2 Samuel 12:14). But what shocked me was the prideful responses of other independent Baptist pastors. Angry name calling and ridiculous rants against the media followed.

We don't do ourselves or the name of Christ any favors by sweeping abuse under the rug or by lashing out against those who call abuse what it is. Rather than retaliating against accusations, we should work to build true purity and godliness in our churches.

While I am a proponent for ministry policies that guard against allowing situations where abuse could take place, standards and policies alone don't change hearts. We need to personally practice and emphasize in our preaching the importance of the Spirit-filled life. We need to report every instance of abuse. And when hiring or referring people to a new ministry position, we need to be both thorough in questions and honest in answers.

OUR CONVICTION AGAINST FOOLISH QUESTIONS AND GOSSIP

There is an old story about a farmer who was determined to have an immaculate farm without one single weed:

> He made up his mind that there wouldn't be a weed on his entire farm. But try as he may, he could not keep all the weeds off the place. He hired additional help, but they still had some weeds. He finally hired enough help and worked long enough day after day so that there was not a single weed on the entire place. By this time spring

and summer had come and gone, and it was harvest time. Suddenly the farmer realized that, though his fields were clean and he could boast in the fact that there wasn't a single weed to be found on the entire place, he had no crop to harvest. He and his workers had been so busy pulling weeds that they didn't take time to sow any seeds.[2]

Most divisive and issue-oriented leaders point out weeds at the peril of their own fruitfulness in ministry. If we can study and learn about real doctrinal issues and work out our response to contemporary theology, that's great—even needful. But let's not be drawn in to "foolish and unlearned questions," which 2 Timothy 2:23–24 instructs us to "avoid . . . knowing that they do gender strifes." (2 Timothy 2:23).

Let's be careful of writing off a pastor who has veered into some unwise association or identity but is still formulating his philosophy and humbly seeking to grow through counsel. Often we jump to conclusions. First Corinthians 13 specifically tells us that charity "believeth all things, hopeth all things." What if, rather than assuming the worst—both in motives and direction—we actually practiced 1 Corinthians 13:4–7 toward others? "Charity suffereth long, and is kind; charity envieth not; charity vaunteth not itself, is not puffed up, Doth not behave itself unseemly, seeketh not her own, is not easily provoked, thinketh no evil; Rejoiceth not in iniquity, but rejoiceth in the truth; Beareth all things, believeth all things, hopeth all things, endureth all things."

In the booklet *Unnecessary Divisions among Fundamentalists,* Curtis Hutson wrote, "Every sincere Christian should be governed by Bible principles and not personalities or preferences. One's loyalty should be to Christ and the Bible, not to personalities or institutions. The question

---

2   Curtis Hutson, *Unnecessary Divisions among Fundamentalists* (Murfreesboro, TN: Sword of the Lord Publishers, 1990), 21.

should not be: who is taking this position? The question should be: is this position scriptural?"[3]

Paul called separations over personalities for what they were—carnal. "For while one saith, I am of Paul; and another, I am of Apollos; are ye not carnal?" (1 Corinthians 3:4).

Pray for other pastors. When you have a concern, go to them personally. We pastors can be worse gossips than those we preach against. And it doesn't always happen in person. Some of it is in thinly veiled remarks on blogs and social media.

Allow other pastors room to grow. I remember hearing Curtis Hutson share how, in his early years, he was not premillenial in his eschatology. But he was influenced by those who were. He studied and eventually changed both his position and his preaching to match his better understanding of Scripture. I'm thankful that men around him gave him room to grow and invested in teaching rather than writing him off. I want to do the same for others.

OUR CONVICTION TO STRENGTHEN
OUR BRETHREN IN MINISTRY

Most men have a desire for encouragement. When this is not found or given, most are prone to wander. This is compounded if a man has a mentor fail morally or display a venomous spirit.

Tragically, the lives and ministries of those who leave their heritage out of frustration usually became reactionary to the negative trends or experiences they have felt. And there will always be those leaders who will coddle and promote those who have been burned or felt controlled.

---

3   Ibid., 11–12.

Interestingly, however, it often appears these great "healers" or grace-giving leaders also have an angle in the game.

So what should we do to reverse those trends? Purpose to encourage one another—especially younger pastors.

Model godly joy in ministry. If you are always angry and frustrated, why would a younger pastor want to learn from you?

Support decisions with Scripture, and admit preferences. It's okay to have preferences. But it goes a long way when you simply acknowledge that the matter is indeed a preference.

Allow for differences that don't violate your convictions. Don't write someone off just because they have their midweek service on Thursday rather than Wednesday, or, for that matter, because they hold their small group adult Bible classes on Wednesday evenings rather than on Sunday mornings. Sometimes veteran leaders see new and different techniques and interpret them as new and different values. That's usually not the case.

Seek to encourage a young leader's family. When you know of a leader going through a tough time, know that their family is going through a tough time as well. Send a gift card for a family pizza night. If you live nearby, offer to watch the kids so the couple can go out for an evening. Look for ways to be a blessing.

Send books or encouragement. If you're always harping about what another leader doesn't do in your preaching and making consistent passive-aggressive comments on social media, don't be surprised if he isn't inclined to listen to your input. But if you pray for him and send him occasional notes to let him know and perhaps a book that has been an encouragement to you, you might actually build a relationship through which you'll have opportunity to provide mentoring.

KEEP THE FAITH

Perhaps the most encouraging takeaway from the admonition Christ gave to the church at Sardis in Revelation 3 is that He gave it at all. In those verses, as He challenges His people to "strengthen the things which remain," we see God's willingness to restore. His instructions are words of hope to a church that was once vibrant in its faith but now faltering in its love and loyalty for Christ.

I still hunger for revival in my generation. I'm not necessarily looking for a revival of fundamentalism, although I believe that fundamental doctrine is essential to New Testament church ministry. And I'm not looking for a revival of a movement, although I am grateful for my heritage and want to pass it on to those coming behind me.

But I hunger for a revival of God's Word, of hearts stirred for God, of souls saved. Like you, I pray with the psalmist, "Wilt thou not revive us again: that thy people may rejoice in thee?" (Psalm 85:6).

I pray that we will hear and heed Christ's Word to "Be watchful, and strengthen the things which remain" and will "Remember therefore how thou hast received and heard, and hold fast, and repent" (Revelation 3:2–3). And I pray that we will determine to "earnestly contend for the faith which was once delivered unto the saints" (Jude 3).

As I consider my journey into and through ministry, I have much to be thankful for. I was called to preach while a teenager at camp. I was blessed with an amazing wife whom I met at a Baptist college. Together we started a church in Southern California and then worked on a church staff in Northern California. For nearly thirty-four years, we have served a church that had twelve members on our first Sunday in 1986 and has been greatly blessed by God since.

As I wrote in *The Road Ahead*, we have seen disappointment, sin, jealousy, and fighting over silly preferences along our journey. But the road that we have endeavored to journey on has been marked by landmarks of truth. These landmarks have not changed, and God's Word has never disappointed. These landmarks have fully solidified my position as a Baptist and have made me thankful I didn't follow the many pastors who seemed trendy along the way. There is a proven path that served the early church and the pastors Titus trained in Crete. It is still trustworthy.

Online communities and social media offer new options for Christians every day—new terms, new methods, new Bibles, new twists on ministry. Not every new method is wrong, but somewhere along the way, we need to pause and consider our direction and the direction of those influencing us. It may be that those with their eyes on Christ, a commitment to biblical doctrine, and a long-range conviction for keeping the faith are not as edgy or trendy as those with more pragmatic methods, short-range results, and fewer doctrinal convictions. But if pleasing Christ is all that matters to us, we will be more attracted to biblical substance than to passing trends.

My mentors passed down some nuances and ideas that could have disheartened me. I've had lots of opportunities to realign, and some have seemingly hoped I would go down a slippery slope. But there was something else my mentors gave me. They gave me "good doctrine" (Proverbs 4:2). So, we can make fun of the idiosyncrasies of our upbringing, Bible college, or early ministry experiences, or we can thank God for the biblical doctrine we have received and determine to keep the faith.

Most readers of this book can trace their lineage back to an imperfect pastor and church who led them to doctrinal truth and personal growth in their relationship with Christ. I believe many Baptists who have been distracted by variant doctrine, unscriptural methods, and trendy methodology are already finding that the leaders of those groups aren't perfect either. Their movements and denominations have weird baggage too.

Personally, I'm fine on the path of the unaffiliated Baptist. I've recently written a new strategic plan for our church, and although we've built over $70 million in buildings, we are now raising funds to build a new children's building. But if our church doesn't grow by another thousand people or if the building program is a flop, I am settled to continue toward the finish line with my eyes on Christ. And if this path leads outside the accepted or trendy circles of compromising ideologies, that's okay. It's not about big numbers, the feeling of achievement, or the praise of others. I am content to please Christ.

This generation of leaders must ask for wisdom and decide carefully. I choose to spend my time loving Christ and seeking the fruit of a Christ-centered life rather than seeking new terms and alliances in order to differentiate from men or movements of my past. At the end of my race, I want to be able to truthfully say, "I have fought a good fight, I have finished my course, I have kept the faith" (2 Timothy 4:7).

BIBLIOGRAPHY AND FURTHER READING

S OME OF THE BOOKS below have already been cited. Others are simply ones that have influenced my research while working on this project. A few are ones I have written that include overlapping or relevant ideas. As I mentioned in the introduction, citing an author (including in this list) does not equal an endorsement of everything the author has written or of everything in the book. But in the spirit of research, I hope these are helpful to you.

Adams, Charles Francis. *The Works of John Adams, Second President of the United States, Volume IV.* Boston: Charles C. Little and James Brown, 1851.

Alcorn, Randy. *The Grace and Truth Paradox: Responding with Christlike Balance.* New York: Multnomah Books, 2003.

Allen, David, *The Atonement: A Biblical, Theological, and Historical Study of the Cross of Christ.* Nashville: B&H Academic, 2019.

Allen, David, and Steve W. Lemke, eds., *Whosoever Will: A Biblical-Theological Critique of Five-Point Calvinism*. Nashville: B&H Publishing Group, 2010.

Ashbrook, John E. *Axioms of Separation*. Painesville: Here I Stand Books, n.d.

Ashbrook, John E. *New Neutralism II: Exposing the Gray of Compromise*. Painesville: Here I Stand Books, 1992.

Bauder, Kevin, and Robert Delnay. *One in Hope and Doctrine: Origins of Baptist Fundamentalism 1870–1950*. Arlington Heights: Regular Baptist Books, 2014.

Beale, David. *Baptist History in England and America: Personalities, Positions, and Practices*. Maitland: Xulon Press, 2018.

Beale, David. *In Pursuit of Purity: American Fundamentalism Since 1850*. Greenville: Unusual Publications, 1986.

Bridges, Jerry. *The Discipline of Grace*. Colorado Springs: NavPress, 1994.

Brown, Michael L. *Hyper-Grace: Exposing the Dangers of the Modern Grace Message*. Lake Mary: Charisma House, 2014.

Chappell, Paul. *Grace for Godly Living: Allowing God's Grace to Produce a Godly Life*. Lancaster: Striving Together Publications, 2009.

Chappell, Paul. *Guided by Grace*. Murfreesboro: Sword of the Lord Publishers, 2000.

Chappell, Paul. *The Road Ahead: Ten Steps to Authentic Ministry for Independent Baptists*. Lancaster: Striving Together Publications, 2013.

Chappell, Paul. *What Is a Biblical Fundamentalist?*. Lancaster: Striving Together Publications, 2005.

Clearwaters, Richard. *The Great Conservative Baptist Compromise*. Minneapolis: Central Seminary, 1963.

Cone, Christopher. *Prolegomena on Biblical Hermeneutics and Method*. 2nd ed. Hurst: Tyndale Seminary Press, 2012.

Dollar, George W. *A History of Fundamentalism in America*. 2nd ed. Sarasota: George W. Dollar, 1983.

Erickson, Millard. *Christian Theology*. 2nd ed. Grand Rapids:
Baker, 1999.

Gass, Mike. *A Glorious Church: A Study of the Origin, Identity, Heritage,
and Integrity of the New Testament Church*. Lancaster: Striving
Together Publications, 2009.

Goetsch, John. *Contemporary Compromise: Standing for Truth in an Age
of Deception*. Lancaster: Striving Together Publications, 2010.

Grudem, Wayne A. *Systematic Theology: An Introduction to Biblical
Doctrine*. Leicester: Inter-Varsity Press; Grand Rapids: Zondervan
Publishing House, 2004.

Guinness, Os. *Prophetic Untimeliness: A Challenge to the Idol of
Relevance*. Grand Rapids: Baker Books, 2005.

Hayek, F. A. *Law, Legislation and Liberty, Volume 2: The Mirage of Social
Justice*. Chicago: University of Chicago Press, 1976.

Hixson, J. B. *Getting the Gospel Wrong: The Evangelical Crisis No One Is
Talking About*. Rev. ed. Duluth: Grace Gospel Press, 2013.

Hughes, R. Kent. *Set Apart: Calling a Worldly Church to a Godly Life*.
Wheaton: Crossway, 2003.

Hutson, Curtis. *Unnecessary Divisions among Fundamentalists*.
Murfreesboro: Sword of the Lord Publishers, 1990.

Jeffress, Robert. *Grace Gone Wild!: Getting a Grip on God's Amazing Gift*.
Colorado Springs: WaterBrook Press, 2005.

Jenkens, C. A. *What Made Me a Baptist*. Watertown: Roger Williams
Heritage Archives, 1901.

Keller, Timothy. *Center Church: Doing Balanced, Gospel-Centered
Ministry in Your City*. Grand Rapids: Zondervan, 2012.

Kinnaman, David, and Gabe Lyons. *unChristian: What a New
Generation Really Thinks about Christianity . . . and Why It Matters*.
Grand Rapids: Baker Books, 2012.

Lightner, Robert. *Sin, the Savior, and Salvation*. Grand Rapids: Kregel
Publications, 1991.

Lutzer, Erwin. *Rescuing the Gospel: The Story and Significance of the Reformation*. Grand Rapids: Baker Books, 2016.

Marsden, George M. *Fundamentalism and American Culture: The Shaping of Twentieth-Century Evangelicalism, 1870–1925*. New York: Oxford University Press, 1980.

Marsden, George M. *Reforming Fundamentalism: Fuller Seminary and the New Evangelicalism*. Grand Rapids: Wm. B. Eerdmans Publishing Company, 1987.

Martinez, Florentino Garcia and Eibert J. C. Tigchelaar. *The Dead Sea Scrolls, Study Edition*. 2 vols. Boston: Brill; Grand Rapids: Wm. B. Eerdmans, 2005.

McLachlan, Douglas R. *Reclaiming Authentic Fundamentalism*. Independence: American Association of Christian Schools, 1993.

McNeal, Reggie. *Missional Renaissance: Changing the Scorecard for the Church*. San Francisco: Jossey-Bass, 2009.

Mohler, R. Albert Jr. *The Gathering Storm: Secularism, Culture and the Church*. Nashville: Nelson Books, 2020.

Mounce, Robert H. *Romans, vol. 27, The New American Commentary*. Nashville: Broadman & Holman Publishers, 1995.

Pickering, Ernest D. *Biblical Separation: The Struggle for a Pure Church*, 2nd ed. Arlington Heights: Regular Baptist press, 2008.

Pickering, Ernest D. *The Tragedy of Compromise: The Origin and Impact of the New Evangelicalism*. Greenville: Bob Jones University Press, 1994.

Rice, John R. *Come out or Stay In*. Nashville: Thomas Nelson, 1974.

Schaffer, Francis A. *The Great Evangelical Disaster*. Wheaton: Crossway, 1984.

Schreiner, Thomas R. *Paul, Apostle of God's Glory in Christ: A Pauline Theology*. Westmont: IVP Academic, 2006.

Sorenson, David H. *Broad is the Way: Fundamentalists Merging into the Evangelical Mainstream*. Kearney: Morris Publishing, 2013.

Spurgeon, Charles Haddon. *Lectures to My Students: A Selection from Addresses Delivered to the Students of the Pastors' College, Metropolitan Tabernacle, London, Volume 2*. New York: Robert Carter & Brothers, 1889.

Telchin, Stan. *Messianic Judaism is not Christianity: A Loving Call to Unity*. Grand Rapids: Chosen Books, a Division of Baker Books, 2004.

Thomas, Major Ian. *The Indwelling Life of Christ: All of Him in All of Me*. New York: Multnomah, 2006.

Vines, Jerry. *Vines: My Life and Ministry*. Nashville: B&H Publishing Group, 2014. Kindle.

Watts, Malcolm. *The Lord Gave the Word: A Study in the History of the Biblical Text*. London: Trinitarian Bible Society, 1998.

Wells, David F. *The Courage to Be Protestant*. Grand Rapids: Wm. B. Eerdmans Publishing Company, 2008.

Wiersbe, Warren W. *The Integrity Crisis*. 2nd ed. Nashville: Thomas Nelson, 1991.

SCRIPTURE INDEX

DR. PAUL CHAPPELL is the senior pastor of Lancaster Baptist Church and president of West Coast Baptist College in Lancaster, California. His biblical vision has led the church to become one of the most dynamic Baptist churches in the nation. For years, the church, which has grown to over eight thousand members, has given more than $1 million annually to foreign missions. West Coast Baptist College has graduated nearly three thousand students serving in gospel ministry around the world.

Dr. Chappell and his wife Terrie have been married for forty years, and they have four married children who are all serving in Christian ministry with their spouses. He enjoys spending time with his family and serving the Lord with a wonderful church family.

Dr. Chappell's preaching is heard on Daily in the Word, a radio program that is broadcast across America. You can find a station listing at paulchappell.com/radio. Additionally, Dr. Chappell is the host of the Spiritual Leadership Podcast, a resource for insightful and practical ministry instruction. The Spiritual Leadership Podcast is available on YouTube, Apple Podcasts, or wherever you listen to podcasts.

You can connect with Dr. Chappell through his blog, Twitter, and Facebook.

paulchappell.com

twitter.com/paulchappell

facebook.com/pastor.paul.chappell

Other books by Paul Chappell . . .

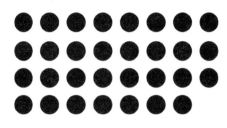

ISBN: 978-1-59894-401-3

To the world, they were fanatics, heretics, narrow-minded
fools . . . outsiders, worthy only of rejection and ridicule. But they
didn't live to please the world; they lived to please Christ. In these
pages, meet fifteen leaders from history who followed Christ and
changed the world. Their testimonies will stir your faith, strengthen
your commitment, and renew your dedication to Christ.

STRIVINGTOGETHER.COM

ALSO AVAILABLE AS AN EBOOK

Other books by Paul Chappell . . .

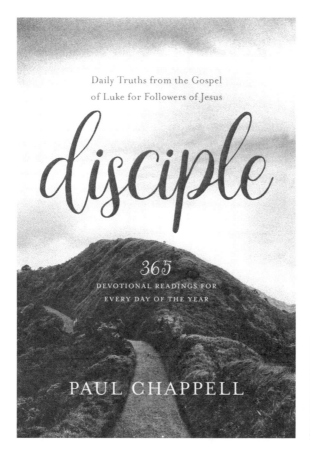

Each daily reading in *Disciple* will take you on a journey through the Gospel of Luke and the chronological account of the life of Christ. The readings conclude with a solid takeaway principle which you can apply to your life immediately. As these brief devotions draw you closer to the Lord, you'll be challenged and encouraged to follow Jesus more closely and to walk with Him in practical ways throughout each day.

STRIVINGTOGETHER.COM

ALSO AVAILABLE AS AN EBOOK

Other books by Paul Chappell . . .

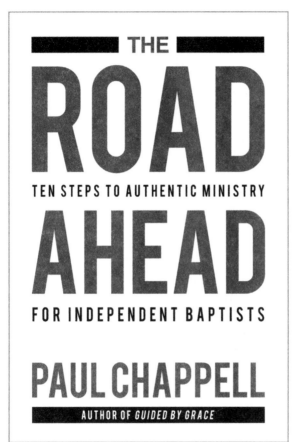

ISBN: 978-1-59894-237-8

If you are a biblical Baptist who cherishes truth, cares about revival, and is concerned for the testimony of Christ, this book is for you. Although we serve in challenging days, the road ahead will be blessed if we make Jesus our target, seek God's face, and are willing to make mid-course adjustments on the journey.

STRIVINGTOGETHER.COM

ALSO AVAILABLE AS AN EBOOK

Other books by Paul Chappell . . .

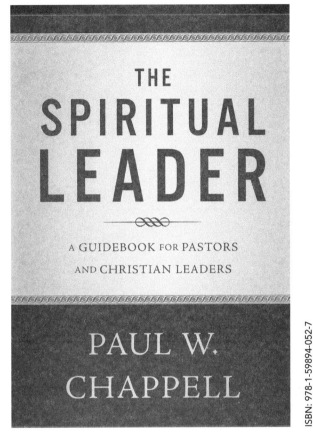

ISBN: 978-1-59894-052-7

Leadership is influence, and spiritual leadership is biblical influence. If God has called you to a position of spiritual leadership, you must embrace the call, anticipate spiritual opposition, and commit to a journey of spiritual growth and oversight. These pages will challenge your heart, equip your life, and inspire you to press on to higher ground as a spiritual leader.

STRIVINGTOGETHER.COM

ALSO AVAILABLE AS AN EBOOK